THE LONG WAY HOME

An Exploration Of Life And Eternity

"For this world is not our permanent home; we are looking forward to a home yet to come"

Hebrews 13:14

"If I find in myself desires which nothing in this world can satisfy, the only logical explanation is that I was made for another world."

CS Lewis

Contents

Introduction

This book is a first for the Fuel Project. In the past, I have written primarily from the head - logic, reason, history and facts. In this book I'm writing from the heart.

That's not to say that it will be any less true.

My hope is that it will resonate with you, and that through it you'll be encouraged and inspired, leaving you excited for the future on this earth, and the one to come.

Mark Fairley
The Fuel Project

Chapter One

Childhood

"It's like you feel homesick for a place that doesn't even exist. Maybe it's like this rite of passage, you know? I don't know, but I miss the idea of it. Maybe that's all family really is. A group of people that miss the same imaginary place."
- Garden State (2004)

It has been said that it's a good thing God keeps the truth of life from the young as they are starting out, for if they knew the struggle of what was to come they may have no heart to start at all. I've often found myself reflecting on just how true that is.

You see, life is hard and it hurts often, and as adults we know that now. But there was a time, back when we were young, when we didn't. There was a time when we each knew nothing of the pain that lay ahead. There was a time when we had absolutely no concept of things like murder, lying, theft, rape, war, natural disasters, terrorism, deceit, greed, heartache and death. In fact, there was a time when we couldn't even conceive that such things were even possible! That time was childhood.

I remember when I was young, (although I can't remember how young exactly...perhaps nine or ten years old) my best friend Brendan brought the word "rape" up in conversation.

He said he'd been hearing it a lot on the news recently and did I know what it meant? It sounded pretty bad. People were going to jail over it. I replied that I had no clue. And I genuinely didn't. I didn't even have a faint idea of what it might be. He didn't either.

It was a couple of days afterwards when he raised the subject again. He told me he'd been speaking to his older brother about it and that he now knew what it was...well, when he relayed the meaning to me I actually couldn't process what I was hearing. I just couldn't conceive that this was even a possibility in life. Firstly, I didn't yet know that men and women could physically do that with their bodies and secondly I couldn't believe that if it could be done, that one might violently coerce another to do it against their will. That kind of depravity just didn't compute in my innocent little mind. In fact, it was so preposterous that I didn't actually believe him. We had a lengthy argument about it as we both tried to process this new information which, if true, would change the way we looked at the world forever. I was adamant that he must be mistaken and that his brother was playing a trick on him. Surely no such thing really goes on?

I was naive, you see. And I guess *'naive'* is the word we would most readily ascribe to young children. In fact, innocence is almost the very definition of what it means to be a child. And what is naivety? Naivety is simply the state of believing the world is better than what it really is.

That's the essence of childhood: to believe the world is better than what it really is. To believe that no-one means you any harm; to imagine that people are always honest, trustworthy and kind; to have no awareness of sin, war, disaster, pain, rape, heartache or even death; and to therefore live for a while in a privileged realm of complete innocence, completely unacquainted with, and likely even shielded from, the harsh realities of life. In fact, this is perhaps the *greatest* privilege of our youth - that for a while at least, we get to live in complete ignorance of evil.

Do you remember what it was like to see the world that way? Do you remember how brilliant you thought life was going to be before you realised there was evil in it? Do you remember what that looked like? What it smelled and tasted like? What it *felt* like? Do you remember how utterly wondrous it all seemed? As the years pass and our younger days fade into the distance behind us, we tend to adapt to reality - we are conformed to it - and it becomes increasingly difficult with all our worldly wisdom and subsequent cynicism to think back with much clarity. But if it's at all possible, I'd like for us to try in this first chapter. I'd like for us to try to remember childhood. I believe our innocence in those days was actually teaching us something hugely important.

This is an invitation to get nostalgic. Let's dwell on the past for a while. Do you remember the home you grew up in, for example? Can you picture it? Walk through the rooms in your mind and let the memories from each one flood back. Do you remember the places you used to go with your friends? What was your best friend's name? What are your memories of hanging out with them? Remember how you used to talk for hours, when you didn't have anywhere else to be? Remember those long summer days at the beach or the park? Maybe your grandparents were around then too. What are your memories of them? Remember going to bed exhausted but happy after swimming in the lake or fishing on the river or playing sports 'til the moon came out? Remember getting into trouble because the ball kept landing in the neighbour's garden? Remember birthday parties? Eating copious amounts of cake. How summer seemed to last forever. The barbecues. Water fights. Running through sprinklers to stay cool. Didn't the world have a sparkle to it back then? Didn't the seasons seem more vibrant somehow? Didn't the colours of Spring and Autumn produce a wondrously intense and atmospheric joy that somehow illuminated your senses? Didn't it seem like the world was full of possibility and hope? Didn't Christmas time seem truly magical? The fairy lights. The glow from the fire. The carols. The anticipation. What did you dream you were going to be when you grew up? Did you dress up as a spaceman or a princess? Remember when there was no stress? Nothing to tax your mind. Just adventures on bikes, tree-houses to build, first crushes to dream about and a world of wonder to explore?

Close your eyes and dwell on those memories for a while. Really focus on what it was like to be a child. Go to the happiest memories you have. Take as long as you need to sink into them...ten minutes, an hour, all day...if specific songs are evocative for you then put them on. Watch old family videos. Take out old photo albums. Just try to remember what childhood meant for you, and as much as possible let the old feelings bubble to the surface. Come back to this book only when you've been thoroughly dowsed in some childhood nostalgia.

Well...did you do it?

Honestly, whenever a book asks me to do something like that, I rarely oblige - I'm too impatient to see what the point of it all was! So I don't blame you if you didn't either. However, since this is so important to where we're headed, let me now take you on a journey through some of my own childhood memories. Hopefully in telling some of my stories and explaining what childhood meant to me, I can help to evoke some memories of your own.

Infinite Possibility

If there's one thing that I remember from my childhood above all else, it's the feeling of infinite possibility. As a kid, I genuinely thought that I could be anything I wanted to be.

My earliest childhood ambition was to become a professional footballer. I *loved* playing football. And like most of my friends, I believed that I was one day destined to become Manchester United's next star striker. For my classmates and I, school break-times were for football, lunch-times were for football, and the classes in between were merely for talking about and organising the next game of football!

The evenings after school were for football too. Most days we'd run home, dump our bags in our bedrooms, get a quick drink of juice and then run straight back out to the playing fields. There were many evenings when we'd play until sunset and there were times when not even nightfall could get in the way. I have fond memories of playing outdoors in near pitch blackness with only a distant streetlight to illuminate the field, shouting for the ball and having no idea if it was heading in my direction until it hit me in the face. I remember a friend shooting the ball at the goal and an argument breaking out as to whether he had scored because no-one was even sure where the ball had gone, let alone whether it had passed between the posts. I remember the evocative smell of grass and wet mud that permeated the air in those days, and the happy, exhausted contentment of trudging home almost every night stinking to high heaven of both. I remember dreaming of what it would be like when I'd be doing all this for real in front of 80,000 fans, and well...when we could actually see the ball!

Football was the one constant ambition but there were others that came and went throughout the years. When I was nine-years-old for example, we did an Outer Space project in school and it briefly inspired me to consider becoming an astronaut. Actually, not even an astronaut...just a guy who lives in space. As part of a class assignment the teacher had asked us to design a futuristic space station...more of a city really...okay, in my head I was basically thinking of the Death Star...and the idea was that by the time we grew up, living in something like that would be a genuine possibility for us. I thought this sounded like a lot of fun and imagined that I would definitely go there one day. (Perhaps during the football off-season when I wasn't too busy scoring goals for Manchester United.)

Maybe a year after the space dream, I briefly wanted to be a pop star. One of the teachers at my school put together a choir and I somehow made the grade. I'm still not sure how. At the compulsory auditions we were asked to sing one of our favourite songs and because I couldn't think of one, I somehow resorted to singing Humpty Dumpty. Even as I sang it, I remember thinking, "Are you really singing about an *egg* right now? *This* is your audition? *An egg??*" Whatever the teacher saw in that audition, I'm glad she saw it, because there was something about the buzz of being backstage, the performing, along with the togetherness that it generated amongst my classmates that I found intoxicating. I hadn't worked out if I could actually sing yet...I mean, except for my Humpty Dumpty which was clearly world-beating...but that didn't seem to matter. I still thought I might just be a pop star.

Not long afterwards, I developed an obsession with jet planes, so I decided I'd join the Royal Air Force. To be honest, dangerous combat missions with ensuing death and destruction didn't really cross my mind at that time; it just seemed like a glamorous life flying supersonic jets through the sky and strutting around in uniforms and aviator sunglasses on the ground. If I'm especially honest here, I was really just imagining myself as a character from Top Gun. However, that dream quickly died when I realised that pilots had to be good at maths. Yuck.

Finally, there was the whole architecture dream. I really wanted to be an architect for a while. I really did. I'll admit that 'architect' doesn't sound so glamorous anymore, especially when placed alongside 'professional footballer', 'astronaut', 'pop star' and 'jet pilot', but that's only because I have presently been encumbered with a knowledge of reality. When I was a boy, it was quite different.

It all started at school when I was assigned an art project to design my dream house. Being an art project rather than a technical project, we were specifically told that there were no limits on what we could produce. No financial constraints, no budgets, no mortgages, no logistical concerns or even laws of Physics to hold us back. The teacher told us that reality didn't exist as far as this project as concerned. We were to be as creative as we liked.

And that's what I loved about it. The limitless possibility. I needed no encouragement to let my imagination run wild. Therefore, my house was simply outrageous. It had a helipad, a grand staircase, indoor balconies, a cinema, an underground football arena and swimming pool, a gym, an elevator, and this was the best part: there was a secret closet in the Master Bedroom on the very top-floor of the house, and behind that closet door were three waterslides feeding down into the subterranean swimming pool. I imagined waking up every morning and instead of having a shower, I'd jump onto my choice of waterslide and zip down it. One of the slides was even designed with a small drop at the end so I could cannonball or flip into the water from a great height. It was a truly magical house.

And here's the important thing: When I was designing that house as a child, it didn't just feel like a fun project to stretch the imagination for me. I mean, the project was fun alright, but the greater part of that fun was derived from my inner belief that I would one day really build this thing. I really thought that. I had a delightfully poor grasp of reality which said to me that if I could dream it up, there was absolutely no reason why, when I was a grown-up, it couldn't become a tangible fact. You see, I thought grown-ups could do anything. Literally anything. And I thought the world itself was just so full of possibility that there would be nothing holding me back.

In fact, I wondered why all the adults I knew weren't building dream houses like this one already. I guessed it was simply because adults somehow forgot how to have fun and stopped caring for things like waterslides. I wouldn't though. When I was older, I would embrace this world of infinite possibility and have as much fun as my imagination could conjure.

Most of the time I didn't even believe I had to wait until I was a grown-up to make my dreams come true. I can't remember exactly how old we were when this scheme was hatched (I'm guessing around eight or nine again) but my best friend Brendan and I once got it into our heads that we were going to build ourselves a car. Two of them actually. One each. Of course, being roughly eight-years-old, neither of us had the first clue about how to build a car, let alone two. But we just liked the idea of it, so we thought we'd get started and figure it out as we went along. The basic concept was to find a scrap yard, grab some bits and then poke around with them in the garage until we figured out how they all clicked together. We'd done Lego before, so we thought it would be a bit like that.

What kind of cars would we build exactly? Well, for inspiration, I dug out an old catalogue in my bedroom containing pictures of remote-controlled cars. Leafing through it together over a glass of juice and a Kit-Kat, Brendan decided he would build a Jaguar Le Mans racer. Not something that resembled a Jaguar Le Mans racer, but an actual Jaguar XJR-9 Le Mans racer - current value around $2 million. I can still remember it clearly, it was purple and white. I guess if you're going to knock together a car it might as well go 200 mph and be purple and white, right?

I, on the other hand, wanted something that would be functional off-road - I loved the thought of driving it to school in the mornings and then scrambling it around the football field at lunchtimes to the amazement of my classmates - so I set my mind on a kind of dune buggy design.

We were so excited about this whole car-building idea that again, we actually wondered why none of our friends had ever thought of it before. It seemed such an obvious thing to do. Who wouldn't want their own car? Why wasn't this a trend yet? In our school we'd had crazes for yo-yos, water guns and fluorescent wrist bands, but why had no-one ever built their own car? This was just baffling to us. Of course, we supposed that once our classmates saw us in our cars they would soon realise how cool they were and it wouldn't be long before they'd all be turning up to school in Aston Martins, Land Rovers and Ferraris too. The teachers wouldn't be able to get a space in the staff parking lot because it would be jam-packed with eight-year-olds hopping out of self-built Lamborghini clones.

For some reason, we never considered that car building might just be impossible for eight-year-olds. Or that the lack of eight-year-olds presently on the roads might be down to such things as laws, driving licences, road tax, fuel and insurance fees. We were completely unencumbered with such nonsense and so nothing ever felt impossible for us. Reality hadn't broken in yet. In our youthful naivety, if we could dream it, we could do it.

With that in mind, it won't surprise you when I say that around this time we also hatched a plan to set up a convenience store in my garage. By "my" garage, I mean my parent's garage of course. And by "convenience store"...well...I actually do mean convenience store. We would stock newspapers, magazines, chocolate, juice, milk and 'old people cereal' mainly. 'Old people cereal' was anything containing fibre. We had noticed that adults seemed to love bland cereals that make you instantly want to go to the bathroom. We didn't question why, we just knew it was true, and that they'd pay money for it.

Of course, we weren't so starry-eyed that we didn't realise there would be *some* problems with setting up a shop in a residential garage. My dad's lawnmower for a start, that sat right in the middle of the room, would take away from the ambience we were aiming for. Not to mention the paint cans. And screenwash. And toolbox. And motor oil. And the family's bikes. And then there was the bare concrete floor and the lack of a working light that made it impossible to see. But we figured if we at least tidied it all up a bit and gave it a sweep, the customers would be able to squeeze by and everything would turn out alright.

When we ran the idea past my parents however, we were shocked by their reaction. They simply laughed and refused to allow it, saying it was impossible and that there were zoning laws. Zoning laws? What were they? That couldn't be right. That can't be a thing. Is it? Brendan and I held an emergency meeting to process this new information. At the end of it, we decided we should forge ahead with the store idea anyway. We figured my parents would change their mind once the cash came rolling in and if these so-called "zoning laws" were in fact, real, we'd cross that bridge when we came to it. Again, we simply thought that whatever we could imagine, we could do. We lived in a world of infinite possibility.

Of course, none of these grand schemes ever made it out of the gate. We didn't build the cars and the furthest we got with the convenience store was sweeping out the garage. But it's fair to say we never consciously gave up on them. I mean, there was never a moment when we sat down and looked each other in the eye and said, "look, these ideas are just a nonsense, aren't they? Building cars? Running business empires? We're never actually going to be able to do this. We're just kids." We always thought we could. Genuinely. And if we couldn't do it right now, we'd simply wait a while until we were more grown up. The more grown up we became, the more possibilities would open up for us.

In the meantime, we would prepare. We would prepare by *playing*.

To Play Is To Prepare

Have you ever watched lion cubs playing together? Lion cubs play by pretending to hunt and tackle each other in the cool of the day. And why do they play like this? Experts tell us that it's not simply because it's fun (although I'm sure that for lion cubs it is most certainly fun), but rather because instinctively they know that one day when they're grown up, they'll be doing it to catch dinner. By rolling around on top each other and chomping at each other's necks, their play in fact indicates the kind of life they expect to live. Indeed, it reveals the kind of life they are *hardwired* to live.

For human kids it's no different.

Brendan and I prepared for owning our cars by testing our driving skills on his go-kart. We would launch ourselves down unfeasibly large hills. In fact, one time we tested ourselves a little too hard, lost control, and ended up flying head first into a hedge. Similarly, we prepared for owning a convenience store by riding our bikes to the shops and buying a variety of chocolate bars. We sampled them and discussed which ones we wanted to stock when the time came. We even used a school project around this time to design our own brand of toilet-inducing cereal called Fruit Bran.[1] We figured we could sell it in our store one day.

Anyone who had seen us playing around in those years - eating chocolate, riding bikes, driving go-karts or drawing pictures - might have assumed we were just messing around, but in our minds our 'play' was always much more serious than that. It was all fun of course, but the greatest part of the fun for us was derived from the belief that we would be doing it for real sometime soon. In our imaginations, all of it was training. Like lion cubs hunting each other to prepare for adulthood, our play was revealing the kind of lives we genuinely expected to live one day.

If we look at the way kids in general play, I believe we get similar insight. Girls will hold a hairbrush in front of a mirror and pretend it's a microphone; they'll dance and have tea parties with friends. Boys will play sport in the street pretending there are 80,000 fans watching; they'll build spaceships or forts with cardboard boxes, turn wash-baskets into boats and pretend they're pirates; girls will nurture dolls and use tablecloths for wedding dresses...and whatever the fantasy they have conjured in their minds, it always reveals something of the child's heart. It reveals something of their hardwiring. It tells us something of the world the child believes they have inherited. Indeed, it tells us the kind of life they expect to one day live.

So what kind of lives *do* they expect to live? Quite simply, a life full of wonderful adventure. Their play reveals that when they grow up, they expect to be weaving through the galaxies of outer space finding new worlds. They believe they'll be embarking on salty expeditions upon the high seas to find buried treasure. They imagine they'll be romanced by their true love and live happily ever after. They believe they'll start families and be surrounded by friendship, warmth and contentment. They imagine they'll have exhilarating moments of euphoria as they strive for goals and fulfil their dreams. And if we were to ever doubt that, we would only have to ask them.

Indeed, go talk to any small child now, any one of them, and ask them what they'll be when they grow up. You'll hear of such grand plans. Stupendous plans. Totally unrealistic plans. But laid out with *total* conviction. Spoken with that unique brand of grave seriousness that only small children and mountain gorillas have really been able to master. You'll hear of all the same ideas. Astronauts, pop stars, dancers, sports stars. It doesn't matter. The point is that they're going to do it. They really are. They are completely, wonderfully and joyously unfettered by reality. There are simply no limits beyond their own imagination. They will be those things when they grow up simply because they think they can be those things, and because that's the kind of world of opportunity they inhabit.

Infinite Fantasy

If there's one thing that reinforces all the natural idealism in a child, it's the stories they hear from an early age.

Personally, I've always loved stories. Every Saturday when I was young, my grandparents from my mum's side used to visit for the day - they'd arrive around lunchtime and stay until evening. When it was bedtime, my older sister, younger brother and I would get into the one bed so that Grandma could come through to tell us all a fairytale - Cinderella, Snow White, Hansel and Gretel...the classics. She knew them all from memory and would give us whichever we preferred. Each of those stories of course, would speak of romance and adventure, princesses finding their prince, true love triumphing over evil, and houses in enchanted woods made of gingerbread and candyfloss.

When she had finished and returned to the living room it was then my Granda's turn to come through for what I considered to be the real highlight of the day. The classic fairytales were often a bit girly for my tastes, and you see that's not even the point. The point is that Granda knew stories about *Fergie*.

Yes, Fergie. Fergie Fergie. *The* Fergie. You don't know about Fergie? I don't blame you because I'm not even sure how Granda came to know about Fergie either. I still don't know if he was a real historical figure or just a figment of his imagination. We guessed he was real. We certainly hoped so. But whatever the truth of it, Fergie was quite simply a hero to us. I'm hazy on the details now but I think Fergie was a soldier of some kind. Maybe a baron or nobleman. A bit like a Scottish Zorro. And he lived in a castle with a drawbridge. That was the best part.

Every week the adventure would begin with a distraught messenger coming across the drawbridge to knock on the door to inform Fergie of some dire injustice in a nearby town. Granda would normally open the story in a rambling, unfocused kind of way to build the tension and we would just be lying there impatiently waiting for the messenger's knock to come. It was all about the knock. The knock at the door meant that things were about to get spicy. Granda would bring the moment to life by literally chapping on the underside of the bedside table and we would jump slightly in anticipation. Fergie would then spring into action, galloping out on his trusty steed to battle the bad guys and save the day.

It was thrilling. Every week we would lie cosied up in bed together while Granda regaled us with the next chapter of the Fergie saga and we would hear of heroism, courage and daring feats, battles won and evil defeated. I remember being completely immersed in these stories and being swept off in my imagination to places far but near, fantastical but true. And I loved the idea that one day soon I'd be writing my own life stories, and that my own life stories might look something like these. I mean, they could if I wanted them to.

Perhaps I'd take a different path. The books I was reading in my own time certainly gave me lots of options. Perhaps I'd become a cowboy and live in the Old West, perhaps I'd take to the high seas to find Caribbean pirate treasure, maybe I'd go on intrepid expeditions to the North Pole. Maybe I'd do it all. I simply loved the way books stirred my imagination and invited me into new worlds.

Movies played their part as well. The thing I enjoyed most about movies was that the stories always ended happily. I guess they introduced me to the idea of bad guys for the first time and told me that a form of evil existed in the world, but crucially the good guys would always triumph over them in the end. To an idealistic child's mind, full of optimism about the future, if there was to be evil in the world then this is exactly how things should play out. I remember hoping to have adventures similar to those of Indiana Jones, Marty McFly, The Goonies or the BMX Bandits.

And then there were video games. I loved video games because I could literally take control of the action and become absorbed by the digital worlds they created. I could decide where the hero would go, how the challenges would be overcome and how the victory would be won. I remember sitting in Brendan's house until the wee hours of the night exploring new continents, scoring goals in World Cup finals, winning wars, solving mysteries, catching bad guys and driving fast cars.

And this was all still training by the way. Whether through books, movies or video games, there was a part of me that always thought, *"this is what the world is really like. These are the kind of adventures you can really have. All you need to do is wait to grow up."* At the very least, I always thought these things would be possible. And I'll go a step further. I didn't just think I could be *anything* I desired when I grew up; I actually thought I could be *everything* I desired. All in the same lifetime. Because in my naivety, I really didn't think life would ever end.

Infinite Time

Solomon wrote that God has "planted eternity in the human heart"[2] and it's true. Children instinctively believe that life is everlasting. Indeed, this has been scientifically proven. Researchers from Boston University conducted studies in 2014 and discovered we are "hardwired to believe we are immortal."[3] And this has an interesting impact on the way children go about their lives.

You see, how much of a resource we think we have dictates how we use it. For example, if we understand that there's an infinite amount of oxygen in the world, we'll never feel the need to become thrifty with our breathing habits. We can be wasteful with our breaths, if that were possible. We can take huge gulps of air knowing there is always more where that came from. However, if we were to suddenly find ourselves locked in an airtight room with a limited oxygen supply, we would quickly become aware that every breath was valuable, and we'd try hard to ration the supply in the best possible way.

In Scotland, where I live, and where tap water is clean and free, we may fill a glass to drink and then throw half away. It doesn't really matter because there's always more where that came from. We can be slightly wasteful with it. Yet if I visited sub-Saharan Africa where clean water can be a scarce resource, my attitude would certainly change and I'd become a lot more frugal.

The same principle applies to the resource of *time*. While adults know that time is limited and therefore treat it carefully, planning, fretting and scheduling to make the most of every day, children who believe life will last forever feel completely at ease squandering the stuff. What I mean is, it doesn't matter to a child if they waste this day or the next...there will always be another one the day after. And curiously, while all the fretting and scheduling causes life to pass by in something like a blur for the adult, the child's more frivolous attitude towards time means that it generally becomes a slow and indulgent thing.

They simply experience life at a different pace. It doesn't so much pass by as meander lazily. Summers last forever. The seasons in general are deep, long and more vivid somehow. Children almost wallow in their everlasting life, not rushing, not worrying, not fretting, not scheduling, but just resting in the glory of it. You'll find kids sitting under shady trees with no-one to see and nowhere to be, and as they do so they're noticing things. Bugs. Clover leafs. The smell of the grass and the soil. They look and they see. Moss. Bees. Colours. The way the shadows appear on the ground. Spiders webs. The way the breeze causes the trees to dance. The smell after the evening rain. They revel in just being alive. They see beauty and they wonder at it. This is why life becomes more vibrant.

For example, do you remember what Autumn felt like as a kid? For me in the United Kingdom it was unbelievably atmospheric. Every year the trees in September seemed to be set ablaze with fiery shades of sunset, flame and glory. There was a first bone-chilling breeze, again normally in late September or early October, that felt melancholic and wistful, whispering through the dying warmth of the sun that change was on the way. It provoked a nostalgia for the ebbing summer, and yet there was a quiet beauty in it all the same. Smoky bonfires and the smell of burning rubber permeated the air and filled the nostrils, leaves fluttered peacefully to the ground, to be scrunched and crunched beneath fleece-lined boots. There were hay bales in golden fields and harvest festivals to announce the consummation of the year's bounty - chestnuts, apples and pumpkin pies. There were fireworks sparkling in the starry skies and in our eyes, while we stood cosily enveloped by big coats and gloves, listening to heart-warming, evocative tales of gunpowder, treason and plot - stories that once again reminded us of evil defeated and of freedom secured.

When Winter was announced by the falling of the first snow in early December, the days to follow would be bright, crisp, cold and white. Mornings would sparkle as the sunlight danced on fresh crystalline ice, and ornamental stalactites would glint and gleam as they decorated the ethereal scene. Bundled up, we'd tumble outdoors, our hearts filled with anticipation and joy. We'd slide down hills and build snowmen and forts, pausing only for a lunch of fresh bread and steaming hot soup. With warmed up insides, the afternoons were defined by rapidly diminishing light and epic snowball fights, waged until entirely exhausted, we'd trudge home contentedly through the night, the snow crunching beneath our feet, the twinkling houses and garden trees now causing the world to frolic in unexpected colour. In the evenings we'd sit wrapped in cosy duvets indoors while gales howled outside, drinking hot chocolate, eating cinnamon buns and feeling thankful for the crackling warmth of the fire. And then there would be carols by candlelight, the shimmering backdrop for wondrous stories of hope and of joy, about a Saviour for the world - an incredible baby boy. Jesus Christ.

Spring would then roll round in March to give life to all our longings for colour and light. The ice would melt while flowers would take bloom, exploding in purples, yellows and greens. The mornings would become dewy, hazy and serene, as if a world that once seemed dead was now waking up from a dream. The sun would grow more benevolent each day and the world would conspire to enchant and delight. Perhaps today the swallows would return, perhaps at dawn we'd hear a new bird song. Maybe we'd see a carpet of bluebells on a forest floor, or daffodils and crocuses outside the door. At school we would draw pictures of lambs and of chicks, reminding us that life was being reborn and that we were abundantly blessed just to be a part of it. We'd eat our hot cross buns, dripping with melted butter or strawberry jam, and with reinvigorated hearts be reminded that Jesus Christ had died for the forgiveness of our sins, meaning this life - this spectacular and extraordinary life - was truly now ours forever if we'd only let him in.

Those endless hazy Summers would soon follow, saturated with a sultry heat and burnished glow. We'd spend hours lying under shady trees, eating ice-cream, looking for shapes in the clouds, swinging from swings and talking about things...no things in particular. The smell of barbecuing meat and freshly cut grass would waft through the air, the buzzing town now alive with fairs, festivals and smiling demeanours. We'd run through sprinklers to cool down and call on our friends. We'd go to the beach, play football at the park, ride our bikes to the meadows and get lost 'til after dark...that's if it ever got dark at all. We'd tell each other stories, spinning them around fires, and at sleepovers no sleeping would be done...at least not until the rising of the sun.

Your childhood may have looked like this or it may have looked very different, but I hope there's something in the description of the innocence of this time that is resonating with you. I hope that it's evoking memories of your own upbringing. And I hope you truly remember what a wondrous place this world once seemed before we realised there was evil in it. Adventure, romance, endless possibility and everlasting life...life is going to be utterly brilliant for a child. It's all going to be utterly brilliant. Therefore, is it any wonder they can't wait to grow up?

In fact, I'll go one step further and say that in a world of such limitless possibility, vivid imagination and infinite time, life can almost begin to feel *magical*. Childhood is a time when a transparent veneer of shimmering fantasy seems to drape itself over everything we see and touch. For a while back there, the line between the possible and the impossible simply does not exist.

All those fairy stories of gingerbread houses in enchanted forests and princes and princesses? They could be true. The notion of a jolly fat man in a red suit who lives at the North Pole with elves and who flies magic reindeer around the world in a single night delivering presents to every single child on planet earth, eating millions of cookies and drinking vats of milk along the way, while squeezing down narrow chimneys despite being twice their circumference, and despite many of the houses of the world not even having chimneys...well that's also extremely feasible too. Very possible indeed.

Don't forget this is also the time when stuffed toys come to life as we sleep. I remember when I was very young going on a trip to the Post Office with my mum. She was pushing me in my pushchair and I had my favourite stuffie, 'Harry Hound', riding alongside me. At some point in the journey, Harry fell out and when I got home and realised he was gone, I was distraught because I thought I'd lost him forever. That was until the doorbell rang and I went outside to see him sitting on the doorstep. *"He must have walked all the way home by himself"*, my parents said while winking to each other. *"Well, of course he did"*, I thought. *"He's a smart dog."*

As an adult, I later discovered that Harry had in fact been handed in by a stranger, then given to my mum, who had played a little game with me, but I was completely taken in by it. I thought it was *completely* feasible that Harry Hound had walked home by himself. The belief in magical stuffies is so common amongst children that Disney Pixar made their most famous film franchise, Toy Story, out of it. Clearly it's an idea that resonates around the world. Oh, and it's not beyond the realm of the possibility that a fairy will visit your house when you lose a tooth either by the way, leaving behind some money if you remember to uphold your end of the time-honoured bargain.

I'm particularly reminded of a day from my childhood when my dad began pointing at the TV and every time he pointed, it would switch on or off. He claimed he was doing it by magic and for a while there, I actually believed him. I mean, I looked for signs of the remote-control and tried to rationalise what was happening in other ways, but when I couldn't figure it out I thought, *"I guess he really has just learned some magic."*

That could have happened. You see, when you believe that nothing is impossible, suddenly everything is possible. The fantastical becomes likely. Enchantment and delight is potentially to be found in every corner.

It's a great feeling when the world looks like that. It makes children so curious to explore. I mean, if you genuinely believe the world is brilliant and full of enchantment, you want to know everything about it, don't you? You want to discover all the wonders it holds.

Infinite Curiosity

Has anyone ever needed to motivate a baby? A baby naturally explores everything it can get at. They laugh with delight when something unexpected happens. They giggle uncontrollably at a new funny sound. Even as they grow into toddlers, they naturally poke, sniff, eat and wander off to find new colours, shapes, sounds and things, because it's all so amazingly fascinating. When a child learns how to talk, the most common word out of their mouth is "Why?" The root of all this childhood curiosity is simply the belief that everything might just be wonderful. After all, we would have no desire to explore if we didn't believe in the beauty of what we might find. It's our innate belief in beauty that gives us the hope and optimism that naturally stimulates happy dynamism.

When I was a child, my curiosity once led me into a bit of trouble at pre-school. We were all given juice to drink this one day, which was pretty standard, but on this occasion it suddenly struck me that I'd never tried drinking through my ear before. I was curious. Maybe ears could do that? Had anyone ever tried this? Imagine how great it would be if I discovered a dual function for ears! And no-one had ever told me it wasn't possible. Who knew what ears could do? And what might juice taste like if it was drunk through an ear? Only one way to find out....

A minute later, with juice all over the side of my face and down my clothes, and with the teacher giving me a stern telling off for being so silly, my curiosity about ears had largely been satisfied. But there was always something else to be curious about apart from ears. I'd continue to poke, squeeze, prod and put things in my mouth because occasionally you'd do those things and something great would happen.

Even as an adult, when you visit somewhere new, what do you naturally do? You explore it! Why? Because you're secretly hoping that you might turn a corner and see something new, unexpected, breath-taking, beautiful and enchanting. You're optimistically searching out wonder. If you thought it was all a trash-heap, you wouldn't bother leaving the hotel room. Curiosity then, and the happy dynamism it engenders, isn't just a sign of intelligence as is commonly known; it's also a sign of *hope*. Therefore, inversely, this is why when people lose hope - when they become depressed - they tend to become sluggish, lose interest in life, and they stop exploring.

Infinite Idealism

I guess all I'm really trying to say in this chapter is that small children are defined by their *idealism*. Idealism. That's the word that sums it all up. Google defines "idealism" as the "unrealistic belief in or pursuit of perfection." And the point I only want to make here is that all children are born with this "unrealistic belief" that the world is perfect. In their minds and in their hearts, they are imbued with an assumption that they have arrived in a planet full of infinite joy, beauty, hope, love, wonder, adventure, fun, romance and time.

It's not true of course. We know that now. But I must repeat what I said before about this: To have these days of innocence in life, to be naive for just a little while, is a beautiful privilege. I hope that with this journey back to childhood, I've done something to remind you of how wonderful those days could be. Of course, your childhood will likely have looked very different from mine in Scotland, but if I could evoke some happy memories in at least the smallest of ways, or helped you remember the hope you had as a child, then my job will have been done here.

Furthermore, and this is important to end with, even if you had an unfortunate childhood, I hope there's something in all this that still rings true, and that resonates somewhere deep in your soul. At Christmas time we like to share olde-worlde snow scenes of 19th Century characters on horse-drawn carriages, and there are gas-lit lampposts, and little spirals of smoke coming from the chimneys of the houses, and the windows are aglow with candlelight, and perhaps inside there are children playing with hand-carved wooden trains...and we strangely do this even though it bears no relation to a Christmas any of us have ever personally experienced. Why do we do this? I think it's because those images convey a deep truth about the season that resonates with our souls. There's a cosy, idealistic charm in them that somehow encapsulates what we think Christmas should be, even if it's never been that way for us personally. Our hearts are warmed and we're nostalgic for something we never even had. I hope this chapter has done something like that.

But now it's time to move on. Because, as I've kept alluding to, and as we all know already, childhood can't last forever. The poet, Alfred Tennyson famously said that it is better to have loved and lost than to have never loved at all, and it's true, both in the romantic sense in which he spoke and in the sense of which we now speak. It is better that we had our childhood naivety for a while with all its joys and charms, loved it and then lost it, than never have had it at all.

But that doesn't mean the loss of it will be easy. Quite the opposite; losing our innocence is going to be extremely difficult. In the years ahead, as we grow up, we are going to learn that time is *not* infinite at all. Instead, we're going to have to get to grips with the concept of death. We're going to have to learn that we can't be anything we want to be either, because the possibilities ahead of us are *not* infinite. We will eventually encounter lots of pain in the world too. We'll witness evil, terrorism, greed, murders, corruption, wars, natural disasters and so much more. And as we come into contact with these things, it will massively alter the way we view life. It will in many ways devastate us. Indeed, we'll soon realise that there is actually a huge gap between the world we expected as a child and the one we have actually inherited. It will confuse and even depress us. It will occasionally cause us to look back wistfully to our childhoods and long for those old innocent, care-free days before we knew so much. It will, in a sense, all begin to feel quite tragic.

And that is really the foundation of this book. It's to say that losing our innocence was actually a tragic thing. And what's more, a very strange thing too. I have to admit, I find it completely *strange* that when we are forced to see the world for what it really is, it should turn out to be absolutely nothing like the one we expected.

Chapter Two

The Tweenage Years

"Don't Grow Up: It's A Trap!" (Meme)

I read an article in the Guardian newspaper recently by the English satirist Charlie Brooker. He wrote, *"Each night I read stories to a two-year-old to distract him from reality, which being two, he hasn't learned to despise yet. He earnestly believes everything is brilliant. Yesterday he discovered the timeless magic of throwing a fork under the sofa again and again and again. He laughs at the sight of a squirrel. Sometimes he spins on the spot and throws his arms out, shrieking with boundless delight for no reason. What a moron.*

He wants to cling to every crumb of conscious existence, so it's tough to convince him to let go long enough to fall asleep. Bedtime stories ease the transition."[1]

Brooker Jr. hasn't learned about all the evil in the world yet. He still thinks it's all utterly is brilliant. He's still enchanted by it. He's still only two-years-old. Brooker Sr. reckons that until he learns to recognise reality for what it is (and despise it), he will remain something of a moron. Of course he says this affectionately with his tongue firmly planted in his cheek, but underpinning the statement is one of the most difficult questions of parenthood: How long does one continue to protect the child's innocence for? When is the right time to start lowering the shield of protection around them and to let reality seep in?

Obviously not at two-years-old. That would be far too early to start informing Brooker Jr. about the reality of war, corruption and death. But if not at two-years-old, then when? When do you tell them about bullying, abortion or sexually transmitted infections? The truth is that if you're a parent, you'll probably find within yourself a powerful desire to protect innocence in your child forever. Therefore, despite knowing that you're reinforcing a sense of unrealism in them, you'll probably do it for as long as you can.

Perhaps you'll tell them that the tooth fairy really exists, or that their stuffed animals really do come to life at night and can walk home by themselves from the Post Office. Perhaps when the family dog dies you'll shield them from death by telling them he simply went to live on a farm. Perhaps you'll shield them from the awfulness of the news or from adult content on television by restricting their access to it. Perhaps you'll turn on internet filters to make sure they don't come across pornography by mistake.

You'll do all this because you're aware of the benefits that innocence brings and you'll want them to enjoy those benefits for as long as possible. You'll do it because you want them to enjoy a magical start in life, full of joy and optimism and laughter. You'll do it because you understand that long enough will be the days when they'll have to worry about taxes, heartbreak, virus outbreaks, cancer, natural disasters and war. They needn't learn about such things until absolutely necessary. In the short-term, ignorance can be their bliss, and you can help to preserve it. And so preserve it you will. With all your might you'll preserve it. Against bullies. Against Paedophiles. Against anything that threatens to corrupt their soul.

But the strange dichotomy for parents is that they know there will come a day when the shield of protection *must* come down. There *must* come a day when they open up and reveal all the dangers that exist in the real world. Because quite simply, if that day never comes, the child will be left wholly unprepared to survive in it.

I mean, we don't really think that Charlie Brooker Jr. is a moron for believing the world is brilliant at two-years-old, and neither does his dad. But imagine if, nineteen years later, Charlie Brooker were to write a new Guardian article about his son. Imagine Brooker Jr. is now twenty-one years old and his dad writes, *"My son <u>still</u> hasn't lost any of the innocence he had when he was two-years-old. Indeed, he still has no concept of evil whatsoever. As he grew up we shielded him from the reality of life so effectively that he still thinks everything is completely brilliant and he still trusts everyone unconditionally. Therefore, when a scam telesales caller phoned him last week and asked for his credit card details, he just handed them right over without question or pause. The scammers emptied his bank account. He's so gullible. So naive. What a moron."* In this instance, we might actually find ourselves agreeing with him!

We would think that actually Brooker Jr. *should* have become more knowledgeable of the real world by the age of twenty-one. In a sense, we would think that he should have become more cynical by now. More sceptical of people's motives. More distrustful. Harder. Colder. Closed off. We would think that. Of course, we wouldn't use those exact terms - we'd use terms like "knowing", "sophisticated", "aware", "worldly-wise", and "experienced." Those are the "qualities" we'd feel Brooker Jr. should have developed by adulthood. Indeed, we would probably be baffled as to how he had made it to twenty-one years of age *without* maturing in this way.

Similarly, if a four-year-old girl...let's call her Sarah...were to hand over her prized Barbie doll to a stranger and then run off expecting he'll look after it until she comes back, we'd think that is perfectly natural. She's four years old. She has no reason to distrust anyone, and we'd be glad of that fact. Such innocence is winsome and natural in a child that young. However, if on her 21st birthday she were to hand her mobile phone to a stranger because he offered to look after it while she went to the bathroom, and then she came back to discover he'd run off with it, we'd simply think she was daft for having been that optimistic in the first place. Again, we would expect Sarah to be more jaded by twenty-one. How could she not be? We'd perhaps pity her and question her. *"How could you still be so naive? Why aren't you more wary of strangers and their motives by now? You're going to need to learn to be more worldly-wise if you're to survive as a grown-up!"* However we express it, we'd think it was really just time she learned what kind of place the world is, and adapt to it quickly, otherwise she's simply not going to make it here.

In many ways then, we are forced to admit that growing up is a destructive process. It's the destruction of innocence. In fact, if, as we saw earlier, childhood can literally be *defined* by innocence, growing up can just as easily be defined as the destruction of that innocence. Indeed, our estimation of maturity in another person is often measured in direct relation to their knowledge of, and their construction of defensive barriers against evil. Whether it be fraud, theft, lies, envy, greed, murder, racketeering, war, injustice, cruelty, disaster, blackmail, bribery, terrorism, sexual immorality, selfishness, sinful depravity or ultimately death, we only consider an adult to be a man or woman of the world until they know about all these things.

So parents have a tough job on their hands. In a sense they have to actively collaborate in the destruction of their own child's innocence in order to prepare them for adulthood. And if they don't do it, the finger of blame would soon be pointed in their direction. Anyone reading Charlie Brooker's new article might say: *"Well why did you overprotect your child in the first place, Charlie Brooker? You're partly to blame for his bank account being emptied. Why didn't you inform him about the greed and deception of telesales scammers? That's your job."* Similarly, anyone who heard about Sarah's mobile phone being stolen while she was in the bathroom might say, *"Well why didn't Sarah's parents tell her not to trust strangers with valuables like mobile phones? Why didn't they explain to her that strangers are often dishonest and selfish? These are basic survival tips for planet earth, aren't they? To know that evil and sin lurks in hidden places? To walk warily of them? Why didn't the parents tell their kids to construct more emotional walls and to be more cynical? They clearly over-protected her! After all, if a parent's job is to prepare their child for independent life, then it stands to reason that a great portion of that task is to get them ready to face all its dangers."*

Which leads us back to the great and terrible question of parenthood again. When is the right time to start revealing those dangers? On the one hand, the parent wishes the child would never have to grow up and learn about all this pain and evil at all, but on the other hand, they know that things being the way they are, they must tell their children the truth if they're to survive. It's like the old line from Jimmy Stewart's character in *Harvey*: *"You have a lot to learn and I hope you never learn it."*[2]

The Transition

In the past, the transitional period between childhood innocence and adult knowing was referred to as *adolescence*, or the 'teenage years'. However, it's not quite as simple as that anymore. We have something called *pre-adolescence* now, or the 'tweenage years', and it basically means the transition is starting to happen much earlier than it used to. It's difficult to pin down when pre-adolescence starts and ends but the core of it is generally thought to be between ten and twelve years of age. Some believe it begins as early as eight, and others believe it ends as late as fourteen. Urban Dictionary simply and concisely sums up this fluid period as *"too old for toys, too young for boys."*[3] That definition just means it's when children start to leave their naivety behind and become more knowing about reality, but when they're not fully ready for all that reality entails.

It's interesting that this age category didn't exist until very recently and I think its emergence can be explained by the fact that the world is becoming increasingly saturated with immorality. Even the most over-protective parents are now finding it difficult to safeguard their child's innocence and it simply can't be sustained for as long as it could in generations gone by - especially since we now live in the "Information Age".

It's now believed that between the ages of 5-15, American children will on average, be exposed to the killing of 13,000 people on television. That's a lot of death to absorb. Similarly, in a typical year on primetime television, a viewer will witness 5,000 murders, rapes, beatings and stabbings, as well as 1,300 acts of adultery and 2,700 sexually aggressive comments.4 If these stats are correct, it simply means that if you have a TV, you can't get to fifteen-years-old in the United States with your innocence in intact anymore - it's impossible. Indeed, you most likely can't even get halfway to fifteen.

And that's just television. The rise of the internet and mobile technology is perhaps primarily responsible for the way in which kids are now exposed to evil at earlier ages. Almost any kind of material can now be accessed by curious kids with a few clicks of a mouse. Indeed, they are often now unwittingly exposed to things they weren't even looking for, and which otherwise wouldn't have been available to them. They see sexually explicit forms of advertising popping up on their screens. They see their favourite celebrities posting nude Instagram photos and wearing less clothes on the red carpet in a bid to garner attention for their latest movie or album - movies and albums which themselves contain increasingly explicit scenes and lyrics. They unintentionally see reports of wars, natural disasters and terrorist atrocities on social media - even things like innocents being gunned down in broad daylight on the street. They see comedians using crude and irreverent language. They buy video games that prompt them to participate in horror, torture and murder...it goes on and on.

That's not even to mention all the more traditional types of sin that have existed for millennia. Perhaps they see their friend's parents are divorcing and they witness the emotional devastation of the fallout. Perhaps they see bullying, or are even victims of it, in the playground. Perhaps they see drunkenness or lewd behaviour on the street. All humans absorb from their surroundings and when the surroundings of children are increasingly saturated with pain, pornography and violence, it's ever-more difficult for parents to stem the tide and to keep it away from their eyes and ears. In fact, it's almost a measure of the moral health of society, to see how long the young can retain their innocence for in it. And if ours were to be measured that way, I think we'd all agree it looks increasingly sick.

So this I believe, is why the "tweenage" age-bracket has emerged. In times gone by, an eight-year-old would have simply been thought of as a kid. Today, we need a new term to describe eight-year-olds because we recognise that even by that age, they're no longer quite as innocent as they were. They're tweenagers. They are becoming aware. And the problem with all this is that in many cases, they're not quite ready for it.

The British television presenter, Nadia Sawalha recently revealed that her eight-year-old daughter had started going to counselling sessions due to an anxiety disorder, after they inadvertently began *"oversharing information about negative world events"* in her presence. Sawalha explained how it happened: *"I think we are really guilty of oversharing, and have only just realised that it's causing problems. Today, and this does make me sad, I'm taking [Kiki] for her first appointment to see somebody for anxiety. I think she has got a really vivid imagination. We talk a lot about the news, we have the newspapers all the time, and she has taken so much of it in. Her anxiety is about safety. They [children] are like sponges."*[5] Sawalha had been talking about terrorism and war to her husband over her child's head, not realising that Kiki was eavesdropping and unable to foresee the traumatising effect it might have on her. In essence, it was eroding her innocence before she was ready to cope with it.

So you see how difficult this stage is for a parent? If they let their child know about reality too early it causes anxiety disorders, and if they let them know about reality too late they'll be taken advantage of by nefarious conmen. The tension of this transitional period means that for a while, parents live a rather strange kind of double-life. They dedicate half of their time to making their child aware of reality so that they can one day cope with it in the world, while dedicating the other half to preserving within them that belief in *unreality*. They enforce idealism with one hand then take some of it away with the other.

For example, they may warn their eight-year-old about talking to strange men or accepting candy from strangers one day, but then as Christmas approaches the next day, they'll encourage them to go sit on a strange man's lap in the mall, accept a candy cane from him, and tell him what they want for Christmas. And they'll do this is in the knowledge that the same strange guy will later be coming into their house unannounced while they're asleep.

The tug-of-war between innocence and knowing will go on for a few years but in the end, everyone knows there can only be one winner. It all must eventually lead to the day when the parent drops all pretence and admits what the child is already slowly coming to suspect - that life is hard, it's tough, and it's nothing like what they expected it to be.

The war is rarely lost all at once. Rather, ground is conceded gradually in the form of several watershed chats. There will be the chat about Santa Claus and the Tooth Fairy. There will be the chat when it's revealed that the old family dog didn't go to live on a farm but rather was put down because of illness. There will come the chat about the "birds and the bees" and forming a central part of discussion, warnings of accidental pregnancies, abortions, sexually transmitted infections, infertility and heartbreak. There will come the day when grandma will get sick and the parents will have to explain that she's not going to get better this time - the kindly lady who loved them, doted on them, gave them treats and bedtime stories all through their earliest years...she's going to die soon, and they won't see her again. And in fact, it must be explained that this time will come for us all one day. Parents must go away too. So must we. Life does, in fact, end. Parents will have to explain that between now and then, there will be people out there in the world who will wish them harm, often not even because of anything they'll do...only because there is evil and violence, and because sinful natures manufacture greed, hatred and lust. It will be explained that to survive in all this turmoil, they will be required to trust people less, to put up emotional barriers, to become more wary of human intentions, to become more cynical, more sceptical and harder than they ever thought they'd need to be. With these watershed chats, the overarching and devastating message is gradually absorbed by the child that the time for innocence is ending and will soon be over.

And isn't this all just so tragic?

Isn't it painfully sad that these chats are so necessary? Isn't it terrible that Brooker Jr. for example, who was once a wide-eyed baby full of the joys of life and who saw wonder in squirrels and who revelled in every detail of the wonder of existence will at some stage be *required* to be broken and jaded to give him a chance of survival on earth? Won't it be a wretched moment when that optimistic two-year-old is finally forced to grow up and realise that this place is actually full of terror, pain, heartache, disease, deception, sin and death? Won't it be a sad, sad day when Brooker Jr. finally learns to despise reality, as his father thinks he should? Just as it will be a sad day for all parents everywhere, when they are forced to actively *collaborate* in the destruction of their child's innocence in order to prepare them for adult life.

Parents may compromise and postpone the inevitable - I've heard of some moving their families to the countryside in the hope that rural life will allow their kids an extended childhood, and some will go to extreme lengths to keep their children away from TV, the internet and social media - but in the end the tragedy is that they know that their children *must* have their innocence corrupted. It's not a question of "if" but only a question of "when". What a tragedy. Let it sink in. Children *must* be corrupted. Innocence *must* die. It should be enough to make anyone weep. Especially the parents who are forced to participate in its death.

So tragic, yes. But I'll repeat what I said at the end of Chapter One - this, to me, is all very *strange* too. Let me explain.

The Gap Is Strange

Why is it that growing up *must* automatically mean the destruction of innocence? And the deeper question is, why should such a large gap exist between the world children expect and the one they inherit anyway? Forgive me if I labour this point but it's so key to where we're headed in this book. So let me frame the question in a number of different ways.

Why is it that we should all be born innocent in the first place? Why is it that all babies everywhere - every single baby that has ever been born on planet earth - why should they universally be born with an inflated expectation of life that just doesn't match up to reality? Remember, naivety is simply believing that the world is better than it really is. So why do kids inherently believe the world is better than it really is? Where are they getting these idealistic notions from? Where are they getting their curious ideas of perfection from? *Why* do they think life is eternal? *Why* do they think it's all going to be utterly brilliant? Who told them this? It's all so strange.

If only a few children felt this way then we may have nothing to wonder about, but when it's hardwired into every single child on planet earth, that's when it becomes bizarre. Where does the hardwiring come from? For the materialist - the evolutionist or the atheist - in particular, it really shouldn't make any sense at all. You see, if mankind evolved from within this universe and is merely a by-product of it, then we should all be adapted to reality from birth and we should have no reason to believe in something better. And yet when we come here, we *do* instinctively believe in something better and we discover we aren't at all well adapted to reality! It turns out that children need to be *broken* first before they can adapt to this reality. They need to be *corrupted* to make it on this earth. They get here with this inexplicable expectation that they've inherited a magical and eternal paradise and then discover it doesn't exist at all. That's so weird!

It should arouse our suspicions at least. CS Lewis wrote, *"Creatures are not born with desires unless satisfaction for those desires exists. A baby feels hunger: well, there is such a thing as food. A duckling wants to swim: well, there is such a thing as water. Men feel sexual desire: well, there is such a thing as sex. If I find within myself a desire which no experience in this world can satisfy, the most probable explanation is that I was made for another world."[6]*

And now I think we're getting to the real point of the thing. The question must now be asked, "Since we all seem to enter into this world with innate desires for life that this world doesn't seem to satisfy, could it possibly be that we were made for *another* world??" Incredible as it may sound at first, the inescapable answer, I believe, is, "yes, we were. We were made for another world. Or at least, another *kind* of world." The fact children deeply, instinctively and universally believe in a world that doesn't seem to exist strongly suggests this isn't the world

45

we human beings were made for. And on some level...some extremely deep level within our hearts and souls...we all know it.

If we're tracking so far then this begs one of the biggest questions of all. "What kind of world *were* we made for, if not this one?" And this is when we have to turn to the Bible for answers.

The World We Were Made For

The opening chapters of the Bible explain the kind of world mankind was made for...a *perfect* one. Turn to Genesis and you'll see it describing the creation of something wonderful - a gleaming blue and green marble spinning through infinite space, and within it, all the fine-tuning required for the most pleasant kind of life you can imagine. It describes fresh life-giving rivers, sparkling and tumbling into aquamarine seas. The seas themselves teemed with fish and other forms of marine life. There were lush forests and grasslands again brimming with animals of every kind, and the soil itself produced abundant vegetation and food for all to eat. There were snow-peaked mountains and white sandy beaches beyond, and there were birds flying through skies lit by sun, moon and stars. There was fresh air and vibrant colour. It was simply breath-taking.

The Bible says God then created man and woman and they were the pinnacle of his creation, made in his very own image. He set them down in a garden called Eden, and this was to be their home. It had everything they could have asked for and more. Indeed, when God had finished creating the world the

Bible says he looked at all that he had made, and saw that it was exceedingly *good*. It was *perfect*.

Genesis then goes on to explain why God created mankind. In effect, it tells us the meaning of our existence here. And the meaning of life is threefold. (I'll be referring to 'the threefold meaning of life' frequently from here so remember these!)

Meaning #1 - To Love God

When God first created mankind he said, *"Let us make human beings in our image, to be like us"*[7], and from this verse we see that primarily we were made to live in an intimate relationship with God himself. Notice how God refers to himself as "us" here. Why is he using a plural pronoun to refer to himself? It's because even in the beginning, the Godhead was always composed of three parts - Father, Son and Holy Spirit. This means that even before time began, and before we were created, loving community within the Godhead was intrinsic to his nature. When he created us human beings, we were merely to enter into that pre-existing loving communal relationship with him. We were created 'to be like' him. That's why he chose to make us in his own image. In other words, loving God was to be the first and most important purpose of life.

Because mankind was *hardwired* for this purpose from Eden, it's one of those things that's intrinsic to all our natures from birth. In other words, it's why every single baby born on planet earth comes with a hardwired belief in everlasting life and infinite time...we really are born with eternity in our hearts. It's why we all *innately* have a desire to worship something too; why we all have a yearning to connect with God. It's why we have an *inborn* sense of a spiritual longing in our hearts, and a conscience that gives us a natural belief in good. These are all echoes from Eden if you like. What we innately believe as kids; what we are programmed to believe in from our first breath; tells us something about the kind of paradise world we were originally intended for and the kind of life we were meant to live.

Meaning #2 - To Love Others

If the first meaning of life is to love God, Genesis tells us that the second meaning of life is to love others. After God made the man he said, *"It is not good for man to be alone. I will make a helper who is just right for him."*[8] He then created the woman and said to them both, *"Be fruitful and multiply. Fill the earth and govern it."*[9] From these verses we can see that love for each other, especially within marriage relationships and subsequently families, were designed to be central to our existence too. And indeed, given that all the families of the world would be descendants of these two first human beings, we would effectively all be related to each other in one giant family! Therefore, we were created to love *everyone* as a brother or sister.

And again, we have to grasp this point: because we were *hardwired* for this purpose from Eden, it's another thing that's intrinsic to all our natures today. Children are all born with a sense of romance hardwired into them. It's why little girls automatically and without any outside direction, dream of handsome princes. It's why they pretend tablecloths are wedding dresses and play with dolls. And indeed, it's why all human beings are born with an innate desire to love, be loved, to be fruitful and to multiply. These are some of the most fundamental and empirically verifiable truths of our nature. And they are echoes from Eden.

Meaning #3 - To Govern Well And To Live With Purpose

A third command from Eden tells us what Man and Woman were to do here. God said, *"Fill the earth and govern it. Reign over the fish in the sea, the birds in the sky, and all the animals that scurry along the ground."*[10] The Bible also emphasises our guardianship of the planet when it says, *"The Lord God placed the man in the Garden of Eden to tend over and watch it."*[11]

These verses tell us that mankind wasn't to be idle - we had work to do. Namely, we were to govern the earth wisely, care for creation and spread out to inhabit every corner of it.

What God is commissioning here is exploration, discovery and science. After all, in order to care for creation and to govern it well, we would need to understand more about it, wouldn't we? God is saying here in Genesis, *"Go! Discover the planet I've made and learn about it better. And have fun out there as you go! Enjoy exploring this place, it's utterly amazing I promise you. I can't wait until I see the delight on your faces when you discover this bug I made in Venezuela. Or when you find out what coconuts are and see what I put inside. Oh, and wait 'til you discover chocolate! And zebras! And fluffy rabbits!*

And seasons! And how I made gravity work! And what those sparkling lights are in the night sky! And wait 'til you see what the liquid inside that plant will do for your skin! You're going to love it! Study this place, rule over it well, because I made it all for you."

And again, because all this was *hardwired* into us from Eden, it's still intrinsic to our natures today. All children are born with an innate and natural desire to be curious, explore, have adventures, discover, understand, do productive work, gain knowledge, see the world, govern creation and tame it. And as we mentioned before, they do this within an innate belief in the beauty of what they'll find. They're constantly poking, tasting, smelling and prodding things because they think life will be full of such wonderful surprises.

So where are children getting all their ideas of perfection from? Why are they so idealistic? It's because children come expecting *Eden*. Babies are *hardwired* for Eden. Therefore, what children innately believe in tells us something of the world we were originally designed for. In many ways the kids have it right! Earth *was* meant to be a world of infinite possibility. It *was* meant to be a place of adventure, romance, optimism, hope, fun and glory. And it *was* meant to last forever. CS Lewis was right when he said that creatures aren't born with desires unless satisfaction for those desires exists...every desire we had as an innocent child was designed to be met by an actual reality on earth. Our childlike innocence, dreams, ideals, hopes and fantasies are echoes of the planet God originally designed for us and the kind of lives we were meant to live. That's why I said in

Chapter One that childhood teaches us something very important. It's through childhood that we see echoes from Eden.

Why then, does the world now look very little like the original? Why is there a strange and tragic gap between the world we expected and the world that we actually inherited? How is it that this place - if it was once perfect as the Bible suggests - how is it that it has now been filled with so much pain and suffering? How come so much murder, hatred, pain, rape, disaster, disease and heartache? How come so much toil and strife that it mocks our childhood assumptions and makes them now look so foolishly naive? Well for that, we can blame 'The Fall'.

The Fall

The Bible explains that despite having everything their hearts could desire in Eden, and despite having intimate relationship with God and each other, the man and the woman both sinned against God in this terrible way: They willingly *threw away* their innocence and *chose* to become knowing of evil instead. In other words, they *deliberately* corrupted themselves. As a result, sin entered into paradise and it was destroyed. The threefold meaning of life was corrupted in the process:

1. Firstly, mankind lost his close relationship with God. This is the first and most tragic consequence of The Fall. The Bible talks of how God came to find Adam and Eve in the immediate aftermath of their sin. It says, *"When the cool evening breezes were blowing, the man and his wife heard the Lord God walking about in the garden. So they hid from the Lord God*

among the trees. Then the Lord God called to the man, "Where are you?"[12] This is an almost mournful call from God. It's something like, *"Where did you go? I miss you."* Being omniscient of course, God already knew where they were. His call is simply an expression of his dismay at the severing of their relationship.

2. Relationships with each other were immediately broken too. Instead of loving each other, as was originally designed, it wasn't long before Adam and Eve's children were killing each other in jealousy and rage. Love was no longer central to their lives at all. You see, when the primary relationship with God severs, everything else goes into a tailspin too. Because of their corruption, love was replaced by hatred, and compassion was replaced by lies, theft, adultery and all the others evils that we now consider a normal part of everyday life.

3. As for the third meaning of life - governing well, learning, and living in a worthy cause - well, that fell apart too. Instead of ruling over creation wisely and caring for it, mankind began spending his time focused on foolish, selfish endeavours and becoming consumed by greed, destroying what had been entrusted to their care rather than protecting it. It all turned into something far more messy than was originally intended.

Adam and Eve deliberately choosing corruption over innocence meant that every generation of mankind from that moment on would be cursed to walk the exact same path. We would *all* be forced to walk the path from innocence to corruption, whether we wanted to or not. Adam and Eve's folly would be repeated billions of times over - the first Fall would set off a chain-reaction of mini-falls that would continue in mankind for the rest of time. That's what the journey of childhood to adulthood has now become defined by. How tragic.

How tragic that we all come into this life expecting Eden, hardwired for it even, and then grow up to realise this world is nothing like Eden at all. How terrible we come expecting the world God made and grow up to realise we've actually inherited the world *sin* made. How awful that babies just don't get the memo and are so naive about the reality of things. And how dreadful for parents that they must collaborate in the destruction of their child's innocence to prepare them for the dangers of life on this corrupted earth. How sad that when kids find out the truth too early, they suffer from panic attacks and have to be sent for counselling. It's all pretty heartbreaking.

The philosopher and novelist Aldous Huxley wrote rather eloquently about how functioning in a corrupt world means we must now become corrupted ourselves. He spoke about it in terms of having to acquire a mental illness. He wrote, *"the real hopeless victims of mental illness are to be found among those who appear to be most normal. Many of them are normal because they are so well adjusted to our mode of existence, because their human voice has been silenced so early in their lives, that they do not even struggle or suffer or develop symptoms as the neurotic does. They are normal not in what may be called the absolute sense of the word; they are normal only in relation to a profoundly abnormal society. Their perfect adjustment to that abnormal society is a measure of their mental sickness. These millions of abnormally normal people, living without fuss in a society to which, if they were fully human beings, they ought to not be adjusted."*[13]

Huxley was in violent reaction to his environment. He could tell that something was wrong here. But since he was an atheist, I wonder if he ever considered the incoherence of his position. Atheists you see, have no right to react violently to the pain in the world. After all, survival of the fittest, selfish genes and violence of the strong against the weak is literally the underpinning of the evolutionary worldview, and if this world is all there is and ever was, then he should have no right to feel so out of place in it, or imagine that it should have been something better.

CS Lewis talked about his days as an atheist saying, *"My argument against God was that the universe seemed so cruel and unjust. But how had I got this idea of just and unjust? A man does not call a line crooked unless he has some idea of a straight line. What was I comparing this universe with when I called it unjust? If the whole show was bad and senseless from A to Z, so to speak, why did I, who was supposed to be part of the show, find myself in such violent reaction to it? A man feels wet when he falls into water, because man is not a water animal: a fish would not feel wet...Consequently atheism turns out to be too simple. If the whole universe has no meaning, we should never have found out that it has no meaning: just as, if there were no light in the universe and therefore no creatures with eyes, we should never know it was dark. Dark would be a word without meaning."[14]*

Why did Huxley feel 'wet', to use Lewis' analogy, here on earth? Why did he feel like he was out of place here? In order for us to feel like something is wrong in this world, we must have some innate idea of one that is better. Where do we get that idea from? What are we comparing this fallen world with? Of course, Christians know that we're comparing this world with a lost reality called Eden - that's what's haunting us. We have echoes of that lost paradise plaguing our souls. We can't help but long for it. We yearn for Eden. We ache for it. We haven't even seen it but in our hearts we're homesick for it. The Welsh have a great word for this kind of homesickness: *Hiraeth*. There's no direct translation for it in English but the University of Wales defines it as *"homesickness tinged with grief or sadness over the lost or departed. It is a mix of longing, yearning, nostalgia, wistfulness, or an earnest desire for home."* We have hiraeth for Eden.

Indeed, due to our hardwiring for it, even the atheist experiences hiraeth for Eden, but crucially he can't explain why. In the movie *Garden State*, it says, *"It's like you feel homesick for a place that doesn't even exist. Maybe it's like this rite of passage...I don't know, but I miss the idea of it. Maybe that's all family really is. A group of people that miss the same imaginary place."*[15] The atheist is haunted with hiraeth but he supposes the place his soul aches for must be imaginary. He thinks the place he's homesick for can't exist and never did. But the Christian knows better. The Christian knows it really existed once. It really did. Therefore, our instinctive, childlike desires weren't lying. Our naivety, our innocence, was actually telling us the *truth*.

If we were to think too long about what we've lost, it wouldn't be long before melancholic hiraeth would set in. We could easily get so nostalgic for Eden that we sink into a bit of a depression about it. Knowing that there was something so wondrous for us here; knowing that for a little while, the world once did contain all the sparkle and delight we believed in when we were young, and understanding it's mostly now been destroyed. It's a kind of poverty we now have. *"Poor us who are all now doomed to be broken by the world. Poor us who must all walk the path from innocence to brokenness. Poor us who must let go of our innate hopes and optimism and become corrupted by a corrupted earth. Us who must gradually become less trusting, more jaded and more guarded to survive. Us who must acquire what Huxley called the 'mental illness' to get by."*

If you sometimes look at this world and think you must have got off at the wrong stop because you don't feel like you belong here, you're actually not far off the truth. In the Bible, Peter describes us as 'aliens', 'exiles' and 'foreigners' here. But before we get too despairing about the sheer hopelessness of our current situation, there is one final thing we should all know: Eden is being restored.

The New Earth

You see, all that stuff about The Fall was just the beginning of the story. It was Chapter One of the Bible. It was Genesis. But the Bible goes on from Genesis to tell us an incredible story of redemption. It explains how God didn't leave mankind to mourn in abject misery, but instead he began speaking hope to the world through wise men called 'prophets'.

He told the prophets that he didn't intend for the world to stay ruined forever, but that he was going to redeem the situation. He told them he was going to build a new earth and it would be every bit as dazzling as Eden had been. He said that he would personally open up the way to that promised land, coming down to earth in the form of a man called The Messiah. This Messiah was to be known as The Way, The Truth and The Life. He was to be the gateway, or the door, through which people could live forever on the new planet and it would be devoid of all the evil, pain and suffering that has come to define this one.

History records that the words of the prophets were fulfilled in Jesus Christ of Nazareth around two thousand years ago. Jesus taught frequently about the new kingdom before dying on a cross and rising from the dead to create the way to get there. And when he left he promised, *"When everything is ready, I will come and get you, so that you will always be with me where I am."* [16] He held out his hand and asked all humanity to join him in the new kingdom saying, *"I am the resurrection and the life. Anyone who lives in me will live, even after dying. Everyone who lives in me and believes in me will never ever die."*[17] And I have to say that no more thrilling words have ever been spoken. I mean, when we really meditate on these words, don't the tears fill your eyes with relief and gratitude?

When you think of how desperately forlorn we would be without Jesus, and how there would be nothing for us but a ruined planet; how we would consider Eden to be lost forever and have no chance of ever getting it back; how our lives would be defined by corrupted innocence then death; and how all our childhood dreams would just be in vain; isn't it the most joyous message we could possibly hear, to discover that there's hope after all?

That's what Jesus has done. He's given us our hope back. He's given us our joy back. Our laughter. Our optimism. Our *life.*

"Why Jesus? How could you love us that much? What did we do to deserve this?" "Nothing", is the answer. Absolutely nothing. We can only fall at his feet, thank him and sigh in relief that The Fall isn't how the story ends. Because of him, it's only how the story begins.

As if to whet our appetites and spur us on, the last book of the Bible, Revelation, even affords us intriguing glimpses of what the new earth will look like. Revelation talks of rivers, clear as crystal. It speaks of cities that sparkle like gems. It describes stunning mountains and trees that give food, healing and life. It reveals glimpses of a place that's exciting, vibrant and glorious, free of tears and strife...it's everything we thought this world would be when we first arrived and so much more. Jesus shouts to a weeping planet in the last pages of the Bible, *"Behold, I am making all things new"*[18], and bids us to come be a part of it. The only thing we have to do is say 'yes'. And if we do, the threefold meaning of life will be restored there. Loving relationship with God, loving relationship with each other, and all the fun, adventure, exploration and learning your heart could desire.

What I'm trying to say is that even though we are inevitably doomed to lose our innocence on this earth, because of Jesus, there is no reason why that should mean we lose our hope. There's no reason why we should lose heart. There's no reason why we should become quite as cynical and jaded as many would think. Because of Jesus, all is *not* lost. Life is *not* in vain. There is a real fulfilment for our longings, the place we're homesick for has been remade, and it's right up ahead. Our new home is under construction! It's a brand new earth.

In the knowledge of this, we no longer look backwards and mourn for Eden; instead we look forwards with joyful expectation. We know that all our childhood dreams were telling us something of the truth, and that all those expectations of a thrilling, windswept, adventurous, romantic, love-filled, cosy, warm, glorious life will one day be fulfilled. Therefore, let's get excited. And let's remember the lessons from our childhood as we go.

Remember when the crowds tried to stop children from reaching Jesus, he rebuked them and said, *"Let the children come to me. Don't stop them! For the Kingdom of Heaven belongs to those who are like these children."*[19] What he meant was, children live with something of the faith, trust, innocence and joy that gives us insight, not just into what this world was *meant* to be, but into what the new earth is *going* to be. Our childhood innocence no longer simply points *backwards* to the beginning of time; it also now points us *forwards* to the beginning of the age to come. That's why childhood idealism remains so instructive for us. Our childhood idealism teaches us something about the kind of people we are destined to be forever, and the kind of life we're going to live. In a sense, the destruction of our innocence as we grow up here will be undone there and we will be healed and restored.

Jesus has given us a new context for life then. And the context is this: this world is no longer our home. It was once, but it's been corrupted. We are merely exiles here now. Foreigners. Aliens. We are journeying through with hope in our hearts but we don't belong. Remember how the Israelites had to pass through a wilderness on the way to the Promised Land? It's like that. We're passing through a wilderness en route to our eternal home. The writer to the Hebrews wrote, *"For this world is not our permanent home; we are looking forward to a home yet to come" (Hebrews 13:14)*

The present world will never truly make sense until we learn to see it in the right way: as a long journey, full of trouble and pain, but a journey that is nonetheless, leading us home. And while I opened the book by saying that if the young knew the struggle of the journey, they may have no heart to start on it at all, the truth is that for a Christian, who now knows how the journey ends, we should have all the heart we need to press on and finish the journey well. No-one chooses to be born, and once you are, you simply have to get on with it and do the best you can. But if you are ever threatened to lose heart as you go, remember this, that whatever we endure here, there's a Promised Land up ahead. The journey won't be easy, but it will be worth it. We're all going home!

But oh, let's not underestimate this: the world *will* try to take your heart.

Chapter Three

The Mid Teens

"I don't want to lose heart! I want to believe, as he does." -
Robert the Bruce (Braveheart)

The novelist and playwright, W. Somerset Maugham wrote, *"It's an illusion that youth is happy, an illusion of those who have lost it; but the young know they are wretched for they are full of the truthless ideal which have been instilled into them, and each time they come in contact with the real, they are bruised and wounded. It looks as if they were victims of a conspiracy; for the books they read, ideal by the necessity of selection, and the conversation of their elders, who look back upon the past through a rosy haze of forgetfulness, prepare them for an unreal life. They must discover for themselves that all they have read and all they have been told are lies, lies, lies; and each discovery is another nail driven into the body on the cross of life."*[1]

We can only partly agree with Maugham. Youthful idealism doesn't exist primarily because of the books children read or the things adults tell them, as he supposes; youthful idealism is hardwired in us from birth. All the stories do is confirm what's already there. And all the parents are doing is preserving what's innate. And yet we can agree that Maugham is hitting on a basic fact - that most of the ideals we expected here don't actually exist. At least not here. At least not anymore. So for a while, life can indeed feel like some kind of conspiracy. Or as he puts it, "lies, lies, lies."

And I love the metaphor of bruising and wounding that he uses to describe our encounters with reality. I've personally always thought of it that way and I can't think of any better way to express it. Every time an idealistic child comes into contact with a harsh reality, it's like taking a fierce punch to the soul. We are left slightly damaged emotionally or mentally by the experience. We are left reeling somehow, wounded in our innermost being and perhaps even crushed in our spirit.

There's a great speech in the film, *Rocky Balboa,* that uses the same metaphor. Rocky's having a watershed chat with his son about life. He says, *"Let me tell you something you already know. The world ain't all sunshine and rainbows. It's a very mean and nasty place and I don't care how tough you are, it will beat you to your knees and keep you there permanently if you let it. You, me, or nobody is going to hit as hard as life. But it ain't about how hard you hit. It's about how hard you can get hit and keep moving forward - how much you can take and keep moving forward. That's how winning is done!"*[2]

Watershed chats tend to come around the time the child is beginning to work it out for themselves anyway - that's generally when a parent knows it's time to come clean. Here, Rocky is only telling his boy what he has already discovered just by virtue of living through his teens - that the world is, despite his earliest expectations, a mean and nasty place. And so the success of his life will largely now depend on this quality alone: Resilience. Tenacity. An indomitable spirit. In other words, his ability to absorb disappointments and hurts and tragedies and pain while maintaining the resolve to keep moving forward i.e. to keep hoping, trusting and trying even when all seems lost. Rocky tells his son that he will win at life in the same way that a boxer wins in the ring: by never giving up. By never, ever, ever, giving up. The boy's got to learn how to take blow after blow after blow without dropping to his knees. Or if he is to drop to his knees, he must always find the strength to get up again and keep going. Will he have the inner determination and grit to do that when life is hard? The answer to that question will define the course of his entire life.

I'm reminded of another scene from *The Last Samurai*. In this movie, Tom Cruise plays a 19th Century American soldier called Nathan Algren who is taken captive by samurai warriors in Japan. The samurai chief allows him a certain amount of freedom to wander through their village as long as he is accompanied by a guard, and on one of these strolls he notices two boys practicing their sword-fighting techniques with pieces of wood in the pouring rain (kids preparing for adulthood again!). When the defeated boy has his "sword" knocked out of his hand and into the mud, Algren goes to pick it up and hand it back, but instead of receiving it, the child encourages Algren to test his skills in a duel with the victorious boy. Algren accepts the friendly challenge and without exerting much effort, mainly due to his superior size, he wins easily.

As this is all taking place, a group of hostile adult samurai warriors have noticed what's going on and the leader of the group demands that Algren stop 'beating up' the kids and drop his sword immediately. Algren senses the tension of the moment but he chooses not to be intimidated. His eyes are filled with determined fire, and so with a steely resolve, he sets himself to earn the respect of his captors by entering into a duel. Algren has got heart, you see. Lots of it. After a tense few moments of staring each other in the eye, the fight begins...and is over again within seconds. Algren doesn't land a single blow. Almost instantly, the samurai strikes him in the stomach and he is brought winded to his knees - the sword swept from his hand in the process. Algren's basic swordplay is no match for that of a trained samurai warrior.

Seeing that Algren is down, the samurai turns to walk away figuring the battle is over. But he has underestimated Algren's determination. Algren catches his breath, picks up his sword and shakily stands up again for round two. So again they fight...but again the duel is over in seconds. This time Algren takes a blow to the head that leaves him flat on his back in the mud. Seeing that Algren looks slightly concussed, the samurai turns to walk away believing that surely now he has been put in his place.

But he hasn't. With blood now streaming from his nose, Algren's heart has *still* got some fight left in it. He comes to his senses, slowly staggers to his feet in defiance, ready to go again. He will not be defeated. He will not give up. The orchestral score underpinning the scene begins to swell to a crescendo in admiration of this heroic yet foolhardy figure who refuses to be beaten. The samurai warrior runs over to him and with a few swift blows, finishes the job. Algren ends up lying face down in the mud. Despite yet another struggle, this time he is so concussed, so sapped of energy, that even though he would like to, he no longer has the strength to stand on his own feet, let alone fight. As he lies twitching in the mud, battered, bruised and dazed, rain still pouring down on him from the skies, he looks about as wretched and pathetic as any human could. The strength has simply been beaten out of him.

The metaphor isn't easily missed - life can do this to anyone. It can beat you to the floor, sap your strength and leave your spirits broken in two if you let it. Ain't nothing going to hit as hard as life.

Life's Blows

Although the tweenage years are when children first get some inkling of what's ahead these days, adolescence is still the time when the full realisation of life hits for most. If all has gone well and innocence has been protected throughout childhood, it's around the teenage years that parents will now voluntarily begin scaling back the shield of protection and let reality seep in. Accepting that the days of innocence can't last forever, they'll begin reluctantly letting their kids stand on their own two feet and give them increasing levels of independence and responsibility. It's nearly time for them to fly the nest and face the world as an adult man or woman now, and a key part of that means they must learn how to absorb life's blows autonomously. So the parents step back...and the blows start coming.

What do these 'blows' of life look like? They really look different for everyone - we'll all fight different battles - and the punches we'll take will range widely in frequency and ferocity. If we're to keep Rocky Balboa's boxing metaphor going, you may think of life's blows as big juddering right hooks *and* small but frequent left jabs.

Some examples of huge blows might be losing a grandparent to cancer or a parent to an unexpected heart attack. It might be a friend being knocked down by a bus. It might be losing a job and suddenly not being able to pay the mortgage or support the family. It might be getting mugged, raped or terrorised in the street. Perhaps it's a husband or wife filing for divorce unexpectedly or discovering an affair. Maybe it's suffering a life-changing injury or developing a disability. Perhaps it's losing a child in tragic circumstances. These are some of life's big catastrophes that can leave us flat on our backs for a while. The worst thing is that many of these things are prone to blindside us on some idle weekday, so without warning, we suddenly find ourselves acutely dazed, confused and filled with a searing inner pain we simply don't know how to handle. Indeed, when these huge tragedies of life occur and our lives seem to shatter, it's not uncommon to wonder if we can possibly go on. They elicit a type of pain so deep that it takes all our energy just to draw our next breath.

The small, everyday 'jabs', on the other hand, are the seemingly insignificant problems of life that, on their own, don't discourage us too much, but over time, the accumulation of them begins to wear us down and sap our energy. Maybe the boiler breaks and you don't have hot water for a week. Maybe a friend forgets about your lunch plans. Maybe someone undermines you. Maybe the kids just won't stop complaining. Maybe you jammed your finger in the door. Maybe all the footage of wars on the news is starting to get you down and the terrorism reports make you a little more fearful about stepping outside the front door. Maybe it's been raining for a week straight and you haven't seen the sun. Maybe you're just a bit lonely right now. Maybe you lost your house keys. You got a puncture. You got the flu. Work is stressful. You saw a sad video on social media. Someone cuts in front of you in a queue or is just rude. Someone lied to you. You know the stuff. We just call it life. There are literally millions of ways in which disappointments and frustrations can build up slowly inside us. If you've ever had one of those days (weeks or years) when nothing seems to be going right and the world seems to be conspiring against you, you'll perhaps know the feeling of your temper gradually beginning to fray or your spirit beginning to break. You'll know how often it can then be a straw that breaks the camel's back.

Remember towards the end of the classic movie, *It's A Wonderful Life*, when life has gradually beaten down the formerly idealistic George Bailey? He comes home in a frustrated rage because Uncle Billy has mislaid some money, but really it's the accumulation of life that has brought him to his wits end. He's so disheartened by the series of disappointments he has faced over the years: he missed his chance to go to college; he wasn't able to travel the world like he hoped and has been stuck in his hometown all his life; he's had to give up on his career ambitions; he's not making much money, and he's lived through the outbreak of World War II...life beats him up so badly that even the sound of his child playing the piano now causes him to lash out in anger. He storms out of the house ready to commit suicide because he just can't take it anymore. This is what life can do. It can get on top of us. "It'll beat you to your knees if you let it."

And it comes at us relentlessly too. Punch after punch after punch. Tragedies, disappointments, struggles, failures and heartaches, near and far, slowly take their toll, day-after-day, week-after-week, year-after-year, turning our idealism to cynicism, our hope to scepticism, our joy to sadness...ever so gradually. Sometimes it happens so stealthily we don't even realise it's happening. It's like death by a thousand cuts. And indeed, it's often the small things that do more damage in the long-run than the big things. Generally speaking, anyone can face an occasional big crisis and after a period of recovery keep going, but it's the day-to-day living that wears many out in the end. It's what we might call the daily grind. The drip, drip, drip of very small but constant, relentless, never-ending disappointments that erodes our zest for life. This is generally how the world strips people of their idealism, steals their joy, and beats them to their knees. Ain't nothing going to hit as hard as life.

Teenage Angst

Now this is essentially what teenage angst is about. Teenagers are notorious for suddenly becoming extremely depressed, surly, rebellious, angry and hard to manage. And this is often confusing to the people around them. Parents may wonder where this new attitude came from and what happened to the happy, helpful child they knew just a year or two ago. It's almost like they've undergone a personality transplant that went awry.

There's really nothing to be confused about.

As the shield of protection around them is being scaled back, teenagers are starting to see the full horror of reality for the first time. It's so much more bleak than the one they first believed in. Where once they saw endless adventure, discovery, opportunity and romance, they are now seeing drudgery, disappointment, struggle, pain, war, corruption and greed.

As these blows start landing, they reel back in confusion and pain, and the first ones are always the toughest to take. Just as boxers develop the ability to take a body punch over time, it takes humans a while to learn how to take a punch to the soul. And so the first few blows are indeed especially dazing.

Teenagers are confused as to why life should start raining blows on them at all. They become increasingly disillusioned about hurtful world they once adored. And they hate it all the more exactly because the memories of childhood idealism are still so fresh in their minds. Those memories now seem to taunt them. This isn't what life was meant to be. They feel betrayed. And they don't yet know how to react constructively either. They can often only retaliate against it all with an unarticulated sense of hopeless rage, frustration and despair. They are grieving for their lost hopes and dreams. They are grieving for their childhood. In a sense, they are grieving for Eden.

Bereavement specialists say that when someone is grieving they will go through five stages - **Denial, Anger, Bargaining, Depression** and **Acceptance.** They say that people rarely move through these stages in a linear fashion but rather they flip in and out of each until they eventually reach that final calm state of acceptance. Teenagers will often go through this bereavement process.

Denial - There will be times when teenagers may refuse to confront the reality in front of them. They may develop an urge to hide away from the world in their bedrooms and to shut everything out. Often they'll go back to the sanctuary of books, movies, video games and music for solace - those places where the childhood ideals can still be found. It's a kind of escapism they're looking for. If they shut the real world out, they can almost pretend it doesn't exist.

Anger - Anger is common too. Living with a teenager may become a tempestuous affair for a while, full of storm-outs and slammed doors. One of the most oft-repeated complaints from teenagers is, "it's not fair!" They know there should have been something more for us here. They'll take it out on parents almost by default, perhaps expressing dismay that they were ever born. Perhaps they will feel betrayed by those parents for having perpetuated the "lies, lies, lies" for so long. *"How could you have lied about Santa for so many years? How could you have kept up the pretence about the tooth fairy?"* In reality, it's not even about Santa or the tooth fairy. The heart's cry is, *"I believed the world was going to be brilliant. You helped sustain the illusion.*

Why didn't you tell me it was all lies?" Indeed, there often comes a nihilistic urge to rebel against all their parents tried to protect at this time. They may actively indulge in destructive behaviour - perhaps even turning to drugs, sex or alcohol for comfort. Nihilistic behaviour stems from sheer hopelessness. As for their books, movies, video games and music, often their preferred choices will have an angry and rebellious undertone, and will be centred on artists who seem to empathise with their pain.

Bargaining - There may be bargaining with parents, or indeed with God. They may ask parents to keep doing things that they should really start doing for themselves. They may bargain to have the shield of protection put back up and will try anything to smooth the road ahead. Many will try to delay the onset of adulthood altogether and stay with parents long after one would expect to see them standing on their own two feet. This is increasingly common as the world deteriorates morally. Adults scared of reality increasingly want to shun responsibility and choose to stay in a state of extended adolescence.

Depression - Depression is probably the best word to describe what many teenagers will go through. They may become overtaken with sadness as they consider the brokenness of the world in front of them. They may become surly and gloomy. They may start sleeping a lot and lose interest in many aspects of life they formerly enjoyed. In the most extreme cases, self-harm or even suicide may pass through their minds. Between 2012-2014, in the 10-14 age bracket, self-harming rose by a massive 70%.[3] This suggests that as the world deteriorates, the gap between

Eden and reality is becoming wider, and so the transition between childhood and adulthood is becoming a more traumatic one to bridge. Self-harming is an obvious and extreme method by which people attempt to cope with intense internal anguish. It's an attempt to physically let the agony out or a way to at least distract them from it. That teenagers are increasingly going to these lengths to cope is a troubling indicator of how traumatic the corrupting process is becoming. They just don't want the world to be this way. They are scared, confused, sad and angry that it is. They are breaking inside in reaction to a broken society. They are acquiring Huxley's 'mental illness'.

These are just some examples of what to expect as teenagers grieve for their childhoods, but as with all bereavements, everyone handles the transition in their own way. Indeed, I don't want to overstate the issue so I should point out that many teenagers will apparently sail through adolescence hardly showing any of the outward symptoms I've just described. The most idealistic children tend to struggle the most, but others are far more pragmatic and will adjust without much fuss. Still others will benefit from strong stabilising influences - a strong family unit, supportive parents, plenty of love and kindness, a strong moral foundation, faith in Jesus, a good network of friends and a positive disposition - all those things can smooth the path immensely and steady a teen's ship when it might otherwise threaten to go under.

Some express their feelings in more constructive ways too, developing an interest in creative pursuits like painting or writing, while others can take out their frustrations on the sports field. Some just have so many fireworks going off inside them that they do things that are downright weird and inexplicable even to themselves. But whatever the coping mechanism, and however the frustration is worked out, it's all explainable as an attempt to come to terms with an unexpectedly broken world.

The System

Perhaps the most intimidating element of the post-Fall world for teenagers is when they become aware of *The System*. What I mean by that is, the laws, legislation, taxes, mortgages, visas, marketplace forces, government initiatives, insurance, litigation, permits, passports, credit agencies, currency conversions, licences, interest rates, CCTV cameras, security agencies, banks, building societies, stock markets, registers, ISA's, bonds, intelligence agencies, administration fees, application forms, planning permission, red tape, bureaucracy, and numerous other forms of restrictions, checks and balances that makes the world go round.

Almost none of that stuff was present in Eden. God didn't tell Adam and Eve to build a stock market or start a bank. We humans have overlaid all that on top of life. And so it all feels slightly alien at first. It's true that we were told to govern the earth in Eden and governance implies at least a rudimentary set of laws. But other than that, the vast majority of The System, and certainly the complex nuances of it, have only arisen in response to The Fall.

You see, when The Fall happened, moral degradation started to creep into society, and like a cancer, moral degradation weakens and consumes that society until it collapses and dies.

Society simply can't survive when it's filled with dishonesty, theft, greed, murder and terror. First there's disorder (i.e. increasing anarchy) and then there's complete disintegration. Recognising that fact, mankind needed to start putting in place structures and supports - scaffolding if you like - to stop it from happening. That's the origin of The System. The System is our attempt to keep some semblance of order and structure in a post-Fall world.

For example, in Eden, when the man and woman were thoroughly selfless, honest and kind, there was no need of legislation coercing them to be selfless, honest and kind. Written laws were only necessary when they became selfish, dishonest and wicked. Likewise, when men and women were innately generous, there was no need for taxes. When they were loving, there was no need for anti-terrorism measures and intelligence agencies. When they cared for creation, there was no need for permits and licences to make sure they were doing things sustainably. When people did right by their neighbours, there was no need for litigation courts. It's only when people started using their freedom to sin, that it became necessary to create complex legal systems, insurance procedures, political structures, economic systems and border controls to resolve disputes, protect the innocent, and keep the whole thing in check.

Again, sin is the origin of The System, certainly as we know it today. It's rooted in The Fall. And every time someone finds a new way to sin within The System or sees a loophole to exploit for their own ends, some new law, initiative or tax has to be introduced to close it. In this way, The System is always evolving to deal with new threats, problems, corruptions and societal dysfunctions. The scaffolding of life is becoming more complex by the day. And more baffling too! Anyone who has done their own tax return recently will attest to that fact.

Kids really have no innate concept of all this stuff. When they make a list of toys they want for Christmas, they have no concept of budgets or monetary values. When they dream of their windswept adventure on the high-seas to Caribbean islands, they don't think about sitting in a governmental office applying for a visa and filling out a passport form, which costs £72.50 in administration fees. They don't even know what a visa is. They aren't thinking about getting their vaccination records up to date, having fingerprints scanned for biometric databases and background checks being run before being allowed to leave the country either. They aren't thinking about the exchange rate, whether they will be able to afford the trip in light of a mortgage they'll have on a house, or whether the interest rate on the boat loan might be prohibitive. The System just does not register in a child's mind until they hit their teenage years. And when we first catch a glimpse of it, it can be discouraging.

What can be especially confusing about The System is that much of it is arbitrary. Theoretically at least, income tax could be set at 10% this year, 15% next year and then 5% the year after that. For much of the United States' early years, income tax didn't actually exist at all. A new law may be signed into effect one year and then twenty years later the exact same law will be completely repealed. To cross some national borders you need a passport but to cross others, you don't. Therefore, not only is The System like a game but it's one where the rules change every day.

And what's more, because it's run by sinful men, it's often at risk of corruption too.

In some developing nations for example, rotten officials exploit The System by taxing people and then instead of spending the money on public improvements as they should, they'll keep it for themselves to spend on private jets and mansions. Since The System exists as scaffolding for society, when even it becomes infected by greed like this, both the scaffolding *and* the society it upholds will soon collapse. For teenagers who are intimidated enough by it to begin with, learning that much of it may be corrupt, is especially dispiriting. After all, what's the point in playing a game where a powerful few have already stacked the deck against you?

Indeed, this is normally why the news is so dispiriting. Turn it on right now and if it's not talking about direct consequences of The Fall (wars, murders, natural disasters, diseases etc.) it's probably talking about corruption within The System. Economies collapsing because of greedy bankers, bent rulers siphoning money to line their own pockets, politicians lying to protect their own interests and then being found out in some great scandal, miscarriages of justice, benefits cheats flouting the law, terrorists beating border controls, traders committing suicide after illicitly losing millions on the stock market, you'll hear about money laundering and forgeries too. The more we see of The System, the more we may lose faith in humanity, the more depressed we may feel, and the more we may begin to feel that we don't want anything to do with it.

Of course, although abandoning society and living off-grid in the woods can be appealing to many, the truth is we don't really have a choice in the matter. If you want to live on planet earth, you have to accept some role in it. The System isn't optional and as the old proverb goes, paying taxes is as sure as death.

The System Is A Game

I found The System difficult to accept when I was a teenager. As a child who had grown up full of idealistic dreams about wonderful adventures, exploring the world, falling in love and living a life free and full of purpose, I saw that The System had the potential to draw me into a life very different from the one I'd imagined.

For a start it seemed that that if I wanted a roof over my head I'd first need to go to a bank and get mortgage on a house and that would instantly put me into massive debt. I'd then have to spend the rest of my life trying to pay off that debt. Since, as the Bible rightly says, *"the borrower is a slave to the lender" (Proverbs 22:7)* I'd effectively then become a lifetime slave to the banks. In other words, I would never be able to stop generating money, for if I did, the bank would take my home away.

To pay off the debt, I'd likely have to take a job I didn't care for. I'd do this job, not because I was passionate about it or because it meant something to me, or because it benefitted anyone, or even because I found it fulfilling, but simply because it would provide me with the money I needed to meet monthly repayments. Money then it seemed, could easily become the central focus of my life. In the quest to generate an endless stream of the stuff to meet the bank's demands, I could easily find myself trading away my entire life for it. Life thereafter could become an endless treadmill of an existence - working, eating, sleeping with no real transcendent purpose - and I could find myself doing something I hated from Monday to Friday every week of my life.

Was this what life would become? Fortunately in Scotland, university education is free, but I saw that in other countries the situation was often even worse. In order to get the job, people would need to rack up a huge debt putting themselves through university, and then they'd work their job just to pay back the debt! It all seemed potentially so self-defeating and circular. Like chasing the wind.

My fears about The System were compounded by the fact most adults I saw seemed to live this way...and seemed to hate it with every ounce of their being.

When I was a teenager I used to catch a public bus to school at about 7:30am every day. I lived about 40 minutes away from the school gate depending on the traffic and since we didn't have dedicated school buses, I caught the same one as the grown-ups as they headed to work.

I remember watching them every morning traipsing onto the bus for their commute and being struck by how heavy-laden they all seemed. I mean, they just looked so world-weary. Like this was the absolute last place in the world they really wanted to be. This was especially true on Monday mornings, and in winter when it was dark and cold, but in general they looked like broken automatons who had been programmed to go through this ritual against their will. Most of them would trudge to their seat, slump in silence and stare out the window into the darkness for the duration of the ride. Often if they did speak it was to mutter to each other about how much they despised Monday mornings, and I couldn't help but think it wasn't Monday they hated...it was their job...the very thing they were giving at least 5/7th's of their lives to. That's an awful lot of life to have consumed by something that was clearly so dispiriting.

I could empathise with them even as a teenager. The truth is I didn't much enjoy the early morning commutes in Winter either. The difference for me though was I knew that school wouldn't last forever. I would have six years of this commuting business and then after graduation, via university, I'd be off into the big wide world on my adventures, falling in love and pursuing a transcendent cause.

Or would I? What scared me was that all these adults probably once felt the same way. They were once wide-eyed kids with big dreams too. And yet here they were, stuck in the drudgery of a daily grind that would, to all intents and purposes, last for the rest of their lives. No wonder they looked so beaten down. Perhaps The System did this to everyone in the end?

Frederick Buechner wrote, *"The world is full of people who seem to have listened to the wrong voice and are now engaged in life-work in which they find no pleasure or purpose and who run the risk of suddenly realising someday that they have spent the only years that they are ever going to get in this world doing something which could not matter less to themselves or anyone else."*[4] And I wondered if the world was full of such people because The System left them with no other choice. Maybe we'd all have the voice of our youth silenced in the end. Maybe we'd all become accountants or administrators or something else that we never intended to be just to pay off our debts. Maybe we'd all somehow end up on a meaningless treadmill of existence because there was simply no other way to survive here. Maybe in this way, real life would somehow pass us *all* by.

I didn't really know for sure, but I did feel that life was too precious to spend each day hating what it had become. Furthermore, I did know that I was desperate not to become one of these broken automatons. As someone who had only recently left childhood behind, I still couldn't help but think, *"Life has to be more than this! It's just too beautiful and precious to waste in drudgery! Life is supposed to be a mind-blowingly beautiful adventure!"* I just couldn't shake that feeling. And what's more, I didn't *want* to shake it. To give up hope of a wonderful tomorrow seemed like giving up on life itself. And so I determined to somehow keep shooting for the stars at any cost.

To be honest, I still think that way today. We all get just one shot at life. Just one shot. And since we'll all pass from this earth in the end, isn't it better to use our brief time here striving to do something worthwhile - even something of eternal significance - than to live in premature defeat like those broken commuters? Isn't it better to commit your life to a meaningful and worthy cause, one that stirs your soul and that leaves a lasting legacy, than to spend life going through motions? As Braveheart succinctly puts it, everyone dies, but not everyone really lives. And on our deathbeds, wouldn't we trade all our days of monotonous safety for just one chance to go back and make the dream come true?

Whatever our attitude is about this, we all need to be careful in our relationship with The System. The truth is that many people grow up to discover they really enjoy being a part of it. And furthermore, they discover that they're great at playing the game. And let's not be mistaken about this - The System *is* a game. Some refer to it as 'The Game of Life'. This belies the fact that not only is it arbitrary, but that it's actually possibly to *win* at it.

You can win at the game. Some people do. Some people just know how to invest in stocks and sell shares at the right time; they know where to buy property and how to maximise profits; they know when to switch between fixed and tracker mortgages; they know how to network and make connections for job promotions; they know how to acquire high status positions. They know how to become, under these terms, 'successful'.

But what would be tragic is, having done all this - having become successful - having done everything right; having traded and networked their way to the top; having acquired the nicest houses, eaten at the best restaurants, clothed themselves in the finest labels, driven the most luxurious cars; having given their whole lives over to winning the game, they wake up one day and discover that actually, none of it really mattered. Realising that actually, it *was* just a game. And that there's nothing of eternal significance to show for it in the end. Realising that they can't take their money with them and that living to accumulate it was actually waste of a life. In fact, perhaps this should be our biggest fear. Not that we might fail, but that we might succeed at things that don't really matter. And so many people do.

Don't get me wrong now, it isn't bad to make money or to spend it. It isn't even bad to enjoy working in The System. But we mustn't mistake it for the meaning of life. The real purpose of life, don't forget, is threefold: to love God, love others, and to live in a worthy cause. If we don't underpin our lives with that truth, we'll get all mixed up. We'll neglect our relationship with God to chase wealth, honour and prestige within The System instead. We'll forget to love others, even our spouses and children, and so neglect them to stay late at the office and over weekends too. We'll lose sight of the fact we should care for the things we've been entrusted to rule over, and so we'll tear down and destroy them instead. When winning in The System at all costs is our aim, we may prioritise money before God, work before family and things before people, and if that's where we end up, the cost has been too high. Not only for the world but for our own souls. We must never mistake The System for life itself.

Where does that attitude get us in the end, after all? Acquiring houses, cars, big-screen televisions and designer clothes is not real success and none of it will matter when life is drawing to a close. Certainly it will not matter in eternity. What will matter is how you loved your Creator, how you loved your family, friends and even strangers, and how you left the world a slightly kinder, more beautiful place to be.

You know the number one regret of people lying on their deathbed? It's that they spent too much time at the office and not enough time getting right with God, and loving people. And yet the mistake is repeated over and over. Why do we never learn? The System is merely the scaffolding for life; it is not life itself. As Jesus himself said, *"Don't store up treasures here on earth, where moths eat them and rust destroys them, and where thieves break in and steal. Store your treasures in heaven...life is more than [your material possessions]" (Matthew 6:19-34)*

Taking On The System

Attaining a balanced view of The System is difficult - especially once we see its arbitrary nature, its flaws and corruptions - but as long as the world is ruled by sinful men, it's the only one we've got. Many teens are so frustrated with it, that they become vulnerable to the lure of anarchy or even Communism at this point, but I won't dignify those with a response. The truth is that democratic capitalism is the least bad kind of scaffolding we have got to prop up society, at least until Jesus returns. Therefore, we have to work with it somehow. And even Jesus encouraged us to oblige The System when he encouraged us to pay our taxes. He said, *"give to Caesar (i.e. the government) what belongs to Caesar (i.e. the government)". (Mark 12:17)* But it still doesn't make it any easier for the teenager when they begin to realise how imperfectly the world is run. They'll still struggle to cope with the fact The System exists at all and that it prohibits them from living quite as freely as they once expected.

Most teenagers will however, work through it. They'll get to a place where they'll think something like: *"Okay, it turns out the world isn't exactly what I thought it would be. And that's a setback, I'll admit. There are obstacles in the way...there are taxes and visas and things. I see that now. But there are still great things to be done. It might take a bit longer to achieve the dream through The System but if I get a job, work hard and save my money, I can still fulfil my goals.*

And as for what I do for work, I don't have to take a meaningless job. I can do something I enjoy. I'm passionate about aviation so I can become a pilot. Okay, it turns out that you can't just jump into a plane and take off like I once thought. I'm in reality about that now. So I'll go to school, I'll study, I'll take a part-time job to pay my way and I'll get my pilot's licence. It won't be easy, but if I put my mind to it then why not?

Or maybe I will be an architect. Yeah, it turns out that architects maybe do have to take into consideration budgets and zoning laws after all, but they still get to design incredible things, right? Maybe we can still live something of the life we dreamed after all here. It's going to be harder than we thought - disappointments and struggles are part of the show and we'll have to learn to cope with that - ain't nothing going to hit as hard as life - but if we show enough resilience and keep going, why can't we still achieve our ambitions? Why can't we still live our dreams, even within the confines of The System? We can win at this game if we play our cards right. And we can do things that matter. And didn't the stories of our childhood tell us that we can overcome adversity and pain to triumph in the end? Maybe this world isn't such a lost cause after all."

For people like us who were, let's remember, never hardwired for this fallen world, we can be remarkably resilient when put to the test. Here in the teenage years the wall of protection from our parents has been scaled back, we've seen the trials ahead, we've taken some blows and disappointments as a result, we've gone through a tumultuous grieving process, but generally speaking we'll recover, get back on our feet and feel ready to take it all on. We're going to win at life. We are going to succeed.

Not everyone will survive beyond this point of course - life will claim some early knockouts. Suicide is in fact, the second leading cause of death in 12-18 year olds. Losing heart kills more teens today than cancer, heart disease, AIDS, birth defects, stroke, pneumonia, influenza and lung disease *combined*.[4] There really ain't nothing going to hit as hard as life. But again, the majority will scrape through their bereavement and find some kind of equilibrium.

First Love

If there's one thing above all others that will help teens through this tough transitional period, it's love. You see, just as our childhood idealism is starting to feel like an illusion; just as we're starting to feel bruised and wounded by life; just as we're starting to feel like we are victims of a conspiracy; just as we're starting to believe that all we have been told about the world from our childhood storybooks are lies, lies, lies, this is generally the time when we first fall in love. And when it happens we discover that it's every bit as magical as we first imagined it to be. If not more so. We discover that at least one expectation from our youth isn't a lie at all.

In fact love is so amazing, it literally causes us to start believing in fairytales and 'happily-ever-afters' again. Dr Seuss wrote that *"You know you're in love when you don't want to fall asleep because reality is finally better than your dreams."*[5] And that quote should remind us of Charlie Brooker's little two-year-old son. Remember how Brooker Jr. didn't want to go to sleep because life was too brilliant to close his eyes? Love resuscitates that feeling. Life suddenly has the potential to be brilliant again.

I was fourteen-years-old when I had my first girlfriend. Her name was Emma and I met her when she started coming to my church. It's fair to say that I was completely overwhelmed when I saw her for the first time. It was a surge of emotion (and no doubt hormones!) I'd never experienced before and had no idea how to handle. She was to me, the most beautiful, fascinating, dizzying, captivating, spectacular, enthralling thing I'd ever set eyes on.

Of course, being a shy and introverted kid, I was a complete embarrassment to myself whenever she was around. I didn't know what to talk to her about...in fact I suddenly realised that I didn't know what girls in general talked about. Normally I'd talk to my guy friends about football and video games. Girls didn't like those things. What did girls like? Actually, what did girls *do* all day? Did they just sit and brush their hair? Did girls have hobbies? I hadn't really thought about it until that moment.

I was so bamboozled by the whole thing that I would actively avoid her for a while because I didn't know what to say when she was around. I was kind of paralysed by how beautiful she was and I just couldn't seem to string a legitimate sentence together in her presence.

One time, I tried to talk to her and somehow I ended up singing. Just singing. Like a weirdo. Another time I knew I'd be getting a car ride with her and her parents so I decided to impress her with some new cologne. I put on so much that her parents started gagging and had to roll the windows down. Another time I was invited to her house for dinner and when her mum served me some carrots I ate one. What I didn't realise was that it was hotter than the surface of the sun, and I caused a complete scene trying to swallow it down before eventually giving up and spitting it out onto the plate.

I just wasn't very good at being in love. What made it worse was that I never really quite understood what girls saw in guys at all - I mean, I'd been around guys a lot and generally found them stinky and unappealing. I could just about see how girls might become infatuated with boyband members and movie stars, but the average ones like me? Why would anyone that beautiful look twice at me?

Despite all the neurosis and random singing, Emma did actually like me and we even went on a date together - my very first one! It was a disaster of course - I still cringe about it to this day. We met in town late one dark, winter evening only to discover there was nothing for fourteen-year-olds to do late in town on dark, winter evenings. As I chastised myself for not figuring that out and planning ahead, we went to McDonalds and sat in silence because I still had no idea what to talk to her about.

So an awkward, mostly silent McDonalds...that was my first date. But you know what? I somehow didn't care that it was a disaster. I mean, I would have preferred if it wasn't and if we'd gotten engaged the next day and lived happily ever after in a castle with a moat and a pet lion, but still...Emma liked me! I was in love. The overwhelming magical, warm, sparkly feelings of joy sustained me for a long time afterwards. Even after the inevitable break-up.

You see, love is an echo from Eden. It's one of those initial commands given in Genesis. It's something we're hardwired for. And it's something that's still utterly brilliant.

There are further echoes from Eden that will sustain a teenager during this time, of course. As far as relationship with God goes, it's still possible to have euphoric moments in worship where they'll feel him right by their side. It's still possible to read his word and know him better each day. As they do so, the puzzling complexities of the world will begin to make sense and it will help calm their troubled hearts.

As far as love of each other goes, not only will they have their first boyfriend or girlfriend but kindness and generosity from friends will bring them comfort and joy. Love from parents will give them security and perhaps even the goodness of strangers will show up in unexpected places.

And as for the third meaning of life - learning, discovering and pursuing a worthy cause - well, it will still be possible to lie flat on their backs for hours under starry night skies and wonder at the universe. They'll still be able to learn new hobbies, explore new places, develop new skills and dream.

What I mean is, there will still be enough echoes from Eden and enough wonders in the world, to keep them hopeful about what this life can be. When life is hitting hard and trying to bring them to their knees, it's things like these that will give them the strength to stand up again and keep going. And as Rocky says, that will be how winning is done.

Chapter Four

The Late Teens

"Scratch the surface of any cynic and you'll find a wounded idealist underneath." - John Ortberg

---

When we talk about "life beating us to our knees" and "losing heart", what exactly does that look like in real terms? If I could sum it up in one sentence, it would be this: We become cynical. Cynicism is the mark of a crushed spirit and a broken heart. The definition of "cynical" is *"bitter, distrustful, contemptuous or pessimistic."*[1] and it's what happens to us naturally as we grow up and encounter the blows of life.

Jeff Bridges perhaps said it best: *"Cynics are just crushed romantics: they've been hurt, they're sensitive, and their cynicism is a shell that's protecting this tiny, dear part of them that's still alive."*[2] He's absolutely right. Since we are all hardwired idealists from birth, cynicism is simply a reaction to the hurt the world has inflicted on us. It's an attempt to put armour around our souls. We all tend towards cynicism as we grow up because we're all constantly being bruised by life. And what's worse, we all tend to feel justified in it too.

Glen Cook said, *"Every ounce of my cynicism is supported by historical precedent."*[3] David Wolf wrote,

"Idealism is what precedes experience; cynicism is what follows."[4] George Bernard Shaw wrote, *"The power of accurate observation is commonly called cynicism by those who have not got it."*[5] Mike Ryoko wrote, *"Show me somebody who is always smiling, always cheerful, always optimistic, and I will show you somebody who hasn't the faintest idea what the heck is really going on."*[6] This is the world's wisdom - that as soon as you discover what reality is like, you should feel perfectly entitled to become embittered by it. Indeed, that it's unavoidable. They say holding onto idealism is only for naive children and fools.

Emotional Wounds and Scabs

It's a bit like this: When we receive a physical wound on our skin, we develop a thing called a scab. As you'll know if you've ever had one, a scab is an ugly, irritating and hard incrustation that forms over the wound to isolate and protect it. It doesn't look attractive but its presence simply indicates underlying trauma. It's like a naturally occurring band-aid or plaster.

Now the exact same thing happens when we are wounded emotionally - we develop emotional 'scabs' around our emotional wounds. What I mean is, we develop ugly, irritating and hard character traits designed to seal off and protect the damaged area. Cynicism is the scab that forms when our childhood idealism becomes traumatised. Here are some examples of how that might happen:

Perhaps one day we open up our heart to a friend to tell them about our deepest hopes and dreams. We hope that they'll affirm those dreams and show enthusiasm and support, but instead, they are insensitive and wound us with some harsh comments. Reeling in pain, we subconsciously decide to put up emotional walls and never let someone know our hearts again. We become bitter towards the one who inflicted the hurt too, and we refuse to forgive them.

Maybe a girl's father keeps promising to be at important events like school concerts or days out so she keeps trusting that he'll be there, but he keeps reneging on those promises and letting her down. Wounded by the constant disappointments, she eventually becomes frustrated and pessimistic of all human nature - perhaps especially men. She decides she can't trust anyone else to come through for her when it counts, and believes that if she wants anything done properly in life, she'll have to do it herself.

Perhaps we enter into a relationship with someone and we dare to love them and hope for a future with them. Perhaps we even get married to them. We then discover that they've been cheating and we are deeply wounded by the betrayal. From that point onwards, we become filled with bitter cynicism about the opposite sex and say things like, "all men/women are the same!" And we refuse to truly love anyone ever again.

Let's say a kid tries to make friends at school and is bullied, being told that she's fat or ugly. Those words cut deep and she develops a hard, aloof, arrogant shell in order to keep people at arm's length from that point onwards. She is full of unforgiveness for those who caused her so much childhood trauma. She reacts to a cold, hard world by becoming cold and hard herself.

See how the blows of life begin to change us? Before long we may discover that we have mutated from an open, trusting, loving, optimistic child to a closed, resentful, suspicious, cold, unforgiving and pessimistic adult. We may find that we are now full of bitterness and that we hardly have a good word to say about another human being at all. We may find ourselves always looking for the worst in others as pre-emptive form of self-defence. And worst of all, we may feel completely justified in all this because "every ounce of my cynicism is supported by historical precedent." With every new tragedy, every new terrorist attack, every new war, every new political scandal, every new relationship breakdown, every new disappointment or failure, we may believe our experience of the corrupted world gives us a right to become hateful of it.

We are often such reactionary beings. *"Oh, that girl doesn't trust me, does she? Well I don't trust her either! And I won't ever again!"*

"Oh, that person is going to be short-tempered and start shouting at me, is he? Well, I've got some pretty choice words to say about him too! Just let me give him a piece of my mind!"

"Oh, that woman doesn't like me and has been gossiping behind my back, has she? Well, I've got some dirt on her too and just wait until everyone hears about it!"

Hurting people hurt people. Wounded people wound people. If someone is bitter to us, we're bitter to them. If someone is mean to us, we become mean to them. Hurting each other all the more. And so all the world becomes colder and harder. There's a self-perpetuating cycle of destruction that works its way throughout society. As it's been said, an eye for an eye in our personal dealings with each other will eventually make the whole world blind.

And this is where Christians are called to break the destructive cycle. Jesus said, *"You've heard it said, 'Love your neighbour' and hate your enemy. But I say, love your enemies! Do good to those who hate you. Bless those who curse you. Pray for those who hurt you. In that way, you will be acting as true children of your Father in heaven." (Matthew 5/Luke 6)* Jesus emphatically tells us not to become cynical or unforgiving in reaction to the world, but rather challenges us to stay soft, warm and kind as a child. Even when the world is wounding us, he implores us to never allow scabs to develop around those wounds.

Remember when Peter asked him, *"Lord, how often should I forgive someone who sins against me? Seven times?"* Peter imagines he's being quite generous with that figure. He assumes that there should come a time when he is perfectly entitled to feel bitter. Perhaps he's even got someone in mind who has kept letting him down recently and he's had about enough. However, if he wanted permission from Jesus to be unforgiving, he's not going to get it. Jesus replies, *"No, not seven times...but seventy times seven!" (Matthew 18:21-22)* Using a Jewish idiom, Jesus is actually saying, *"forgive endlessly, Peter! Never let unforgiveness creep into your heart! Never!"*

Paul wrote, *"Get rid of all bitterness, rage, anger, harsh words, and slander, as well as all types of evil behaviour. Instead, be kind to each other, tenderhearted, forgiving one another, just as God through Christ has forgiven you." (Ephesians 4:31-32)*

He also wrote, *"Since God chose you to be the holy people he loves, you must clothe yourselves with tenderhearted mercy, kindness, humility, gentleness, and patience. Make allowance for each other's faults, and forgive anyone who offends you. Remember, the Lord forgave you, so you must forgive others. Above all, clothe yourselves, with love, which binds us all together in perfect harmony. And let the peace that comes from Christ rule your hearts. For as members of one body you are called to live in peace. And always be thankful."* (Colossians 3:13)

Over and over, we are told that for every wound laid upon us by reality, we need shun bitterness and instead reply with what it calls 'the fruit of the Spirit' - love, joy, peace, patience, kindness, goodness, faithfulness, gentleness and self-control.[6] In other words, don't let cold people produce coldness in you. Don't let their hardness cause you to become hard. Stay warm, stay soft, stay open. In this way, stay *childlike*! Again, notice how Jesus himself connects this message to children. He says that when you forgive enemies, *"you will be acting as true children of your Father in heaven."* And the kingdom belongs to such as these.

Living As Ambassadors of Another Kingdom

Retaining our idealism after losing our innocence is in fact, the *greatest* challenge of adulthood. To keep our hearts open and soft in the face of pain...well, there is nothing more difficult and yet nothing more important. There is nothing harder than forgiving enemies. There is nothing more difficult than continuing to trust and look forward with optimism when people just keep letting us down. And it will take every ounce of courage we have to keep opening up our hearts when they're so often damaged in the process. But I cannot over emphasise how important it is that we do this. Do *not* become cynical. Cynicism is death. Do not lose heart. Because the truth is, we are ambassadors of Christ in all this. We are ambassadors of another world.

That's what Jesus asks of us. Jesus effectively asks us to live as ambassadors of the future kingdom here on earth. Paul writes, *"So we are Christ's ambassadors; God is making his appeal through us." (2 Corinthians 5:20)* God is making his appeal through *us*. In other words, we are to give people a glimpse of what the future kingdom will be like and to bring something of it to earth. In a sense, that kingdom should already be breaking in through us this very second, luring others towards God. To put it another way, we are to be lights that shine in the darkness to illuminate the path home. And we are to be as winsome as innocent children as we do it.

And how can we do that unless a bit of the future kingdom remains alive inside *us*? How can we demonstrate the faith, hope, love and joy that represents the life to come if all that's in us has become bitter, hateful, weary and cold?

We simply cannot. And that's why we simply can't allow ourselves to become cynical. That's why we can't afford to lose heart. And why should we at any rate? Do we really believe that death has been conquered? Do we really believe that evil will be undone in the end? Do we really believe there will be justice? Do we really believe that we are destined to live forever with Christ in a place without suffering or tears? Do we really believe that our heart's ideals will be met someday in the future? If so, then we should *retain* those ideals, not give up on them, and we should stamp them on the world as a sign of the age of the come.

Up until our teenage years, it's all easy. Hope, optimism and joy comes easily. But from our late teens onwards, it becomes a conscious battle. We must actively learn to *choose* optimism over pessimism, hope over fear, forgiveness over resentment, joy over worry and life over death. We must fight this battle every day for the rest of our lives. And we must do it as ambassadors of Christ.

I remember talking with an unbelieving friend about the Christian command to love our enemies and he scoffed and said it just wasn't realistic. He said that no-one could really do that. Later that very night we were watching a crime show on television where a Christian woman had lost her son in a burglary. On camera she said with absolute sincerity that she had forgiven the intruder who killed him, and that she could do it because of her faith in Jesus. I turned to my friend and smiled with a nod of satisfaction. That woman, through her faith, was living as an ambassador of another kingdom in that moment, and on that TV show she had helped to point the way home to my friend.

But what will it be for us? Here's the stark choice we all face as we enter into adulthood: Either we let reality impose upon our idealism and crush it, becoming cynical and embittered in the process, *or* we take that longing for heaven in our hearts; that vision of home; our future kingdom; feed it, nourish it, keep it alive, and then impose it upon reality to make life better for everyone and to point the way home. Either reality changes us *or* we change reality. It's as simple as that. So again, what will it be? We must all decide. And know this, if you choose the latter, you have no idea just what staggering things can be done.

You can do impossible things.

You can change the world.

Chapter Five

Young Adulthood

"Reality can be beaten with enough imagination." - Mark Twain

---

Possibly my greatest hero outside of the Bible is William Wilberforce. I love that man. Wilberforce was a Christian British politician who lived in the 18th and 19th Centuries, and the society he was born into was filled with deep problems.

Due to the Age of Enlightenment, faith in God at that time was weakening and even becoming stigmatised. It was considered irrational fanaticism to adhere to one's faith too enthusiastically, and speaking about Jesus Christ in polite conversation was sure to elicit strong disapproval and rebuke. A bit like our own time, people were expected to 'keep their religion to themselves', and again like today, because God was being marginalised from society, its fabric had begun tearing.

For example, prostitution was rife. Brothels had become acceptable and even quite fashionable. As sexual deviancy became more extreme, paedophilia then became a problem as girls at least as young as twelve started being drawn into the system. Drunkenness had spiralled out of control too, and this was leading to inner-city violence and frequent riots around the country. There was much squalor. Criminals no longer feared the law and so began carrying out their deeds shamelessly in broad daylight. By 1796, it was officially estimated that around one eighth of all the citizens in London were supporting themselves through some form of illegal activity - from prostitution to embezzlement, from thieving to fraud. In short, it was an incredibly debased culture.[1]

Of all the social evils that plagued 18th Century Britain however, by far the worst was the wide acceptance of human trafficking and slavery. Britain had an empire at that time which stretched around the globe. With colonies on every continent, it was called "the empire upon which the sun never sets", and it was believed that this empire simply couldn't survive without the economic advantages of slavery. Therefore, ships would routinely leave Britain for Africa to kidnap human beings, transport them to the colonies, trade them like cattle, and work them to death. The practice was so deeply ingrained into culture that it was considered a normal and routine part of everyday life.

Looking at all this evil in the world, any man might have felt a right to become cynical about it. Indeed, the length, width and depth of the debauchery may have made the idea of tackling it seem rather futile. How could such entrenched cultural wickedness ever be changed? Surely it was impossible? How could anyone hope to reform an empire?

William Wilberforce was born into the middle of it all, and after going through his own transitional teenage struggles as he tried to process the corruption he saw in the world, he emerged in his mid twenties as a young man determined to take all the injustices on. He wrote boldly, *"God Almighty has set before me two great objects: the suppression of the slave trade and the reformation of manners [i.e. morality]."*[2]

And this is the extraordinary thing about Wilberforce: When he came into contact with the bruising, wounding truth of reality, instead of letting it beat him to his knees like everyone else in his era; instead of shrugging and becoming cynical; instead of dropping his idealism and allowing himself to be broken to adapt to a broken world, he did the complete opposite. He held tight to his idealism, anchored it in "God Almighty" and then used it to *fight* reality; indeed to *change* reality. He took that longing for Eden that had been in him since birth; that longing for how things should be; that longing for home; and he imposed it upon his nation. Thus the whole British Empire. Thus the whole world.

He wrote, *"To the decline of Religion and Morality our national difficulties must both directly and indirectly be chiefly ascribed; and my only solid hopes for the well-being of my country depend, not so much on her fleets and armies, not so much on the wisdom of her rulers, or the spirit of her people, as on the persuasion that she still contains many, who love and obey the Gospel of Christ; that their intercessions may yet prevail; that for the sake of these, Heaven may still look upon us with an eye of favour."*[3]

Wilberforce didn't place his hope for transformation in men. His only solid hope was that through Jesus Christ, he could do the impossible. And it *was* impossible really - to transform the world's mightiest empire. But he placed no limits on Jesus' power. He wrote, *"If a principle of true religion should...gain ground, there is no estimating the effects on public morals, and the consequent influence on our national welfare."4*

Over the course of his life then, Wilberforce would constantly fight incredible odds to achieve his two aims. As he campaigned for the abolition of the slave trade throughout the British Empire, he was opposed by the voice of the majority at every step. When he made speeches in parliament about the issue, he was often a lone voice in a sea of hostility. Opponents would yell over him to try to drown him out. Many who thought the British Empire couldn't survive without slavery accused him of sedition and of being a traitor to the crown.

His own health was often no friend either. He endured some serious conditions such as ulcerative colitis and his eyesight was often unreliable too, but he never gave up. He never, ever, ever, gave up. He fought tirelessly for his impossible dream. He fought for it for most of his adult life - around fifty years in total. He fought for it with tenacity, with resilience, with an indomitable spirit, believing that if he took that innate longing for Eden in his soul and imposed it upon the world, reality *could* be changed.

Of course, he had the help of family and friends too. The cynics mockingly called them "The Clapham Sect" or "The Saints". Historian, Stephen Tomkins, wrote that they were, *"a network of friends and families in England, with William Wilberforce as its centre of gravity, who were powerfully bound together by their shared moral and spiritual values, by their religious mission and social activism, by their love for each other, and by marriage."5* Together they worked to reform society by distributing Bibles and tracts wherever they could and establishing initiatives like Sunday schools. One of their number, an itinerant preacher called Thomas Clarkson, travelled around the country campaigning to whoever would listen. They formed societies and used whatever talents they had at their disposal to reach the hearts and minds of the citizens. And you know what? They won. They actually won. They did it. They changed reality.

In 1807, Wilberforce witnessed the Abolition of the Slave Trade Act coming into law, and then on July 26th, 1833, he was able to hear about the passing of the Abolition Bill which ended all slavery in the British Empire. He died just three days later on July 29th, 1833. He had literally given his whole life to the cause but through sheer dogged tenacity, and faith in what Jesus could do through his efforts, he succeeded. The timing of his death suggests to me that God, in his kindness towards a loyal servant, had kept Wilberforce alive just long enough to experience victory in the flesh before calling him home. But either way, he had won.

Not only that, but The Clapham Sect lived to see the whole of society reformed too. Drunkenness and rioting diminished, crime receded, sex was re-sanctified, while a stronger measure of general civility returned to the British Isles. Tomkins goes so far as to say that the ethos of the Clapham Sect became the ethos of the entire age to follow. In short, because of Wilberforce and his friends, millions of human beings were liberated from the chains of subjugation and slavery, and generations to come would live in a cleaner, kinder, happier society.

Even the animals were better off after Wilberforce, as he was the one who established the world's first animal welfare society - today known as the Royal Society For The Prevention of

Cruelty To Animals (RSPCA). Therefore, his was a life that perfectly demonstrated what can be done when we follow the original threefold meaning from Eden and impose it on the fallen world. Firstly, Wilberforce had used his life to truly honour and worship God. Secondly, he had used his life to truly love others in practical ways. And thirdly, he had used his life to truly show wise guardianship over creation. He had done the impossible. And you know what? I bet it was kind of fun. Furthermore, I bet he went home to heaven a contented and happy man.

Idealists Create The Future

Wilberforce is just one example, of course. But when you look at other greats from history, you discover this common trait amongst them: they were *all* idealists. All of them. Every single one. They were all people who didn't just see how the world was; they were people who saw how the world *could* be. They were people who had a vision of something better than reality - whether they realised it or not, they had a vision of home - and instead of letting it be crushed by reality, they worked tirelessly to bring that vision into being.

Indeed, this is what it means to be a visionary. It means to follow a dream even when you have no right to believe it can come true. It means happily trotting off to uncover new horizons without ever knowing if there's anything to be discovered or knowing if it's possible to get there. It means persistence when pessimism in others has caused them to give up. It means nurturing an indomitable optimism within that will compel you to keep wondering, imagining, inventing and risking at all costs.

And it's *only* people like this who change things. Helen Keller said, *"Believe. No pessimist ever discovered the secrets of the stars, or sailed to an uncharted island, or opened a new heaven to the human spirit."*[6] The first step to doing anything great is to have a vision of something better than this fallen reality; to not just see what is, but to see what could be; and subsequently to have the optimism to believe that it's possible to physically bring that vision to life.

Let's look at some other example from history: William Wallace, for example. When King Edward I of England was oppressing Scotland in the 13th Century, the Scottish clan leaders of the day were generally cynical and thought fighting back would be futile - the English simply had a much larger and more powerful army they couldn't hope to defeat. So what did they do? They shrugged and accepted the reality of things. They settled for English occupation. It took the idealistic William Wallace to change things. He said something more like, *"Yes, my countrymen may be oppressed now, but they shouldn't be. I believe in an ideal of freedom. I see a vision of something better. And even though the odds are stacked against us, I will fight for that ideal."* History records that he inspired Scotland to win back its freedom, and in doing so Wallace achieved the impossible dream.

When the cynics saw that there was racial inequality in mid 20th Century America, they shrugged and accepted it. Not everyone liked it but that's the way things were and it was too deeply ingrained in culture to be changed. That was until Martin Luther King Jr. came onto the scene. Here was an idealist who literally said, *"I have a dream! I have a dream that my four little children will one day live in a nation where they will not be judged by the colour of their skin but by the content of their character!"*[7] He had a vision of a better world, he worked peacefully to bring it to life, and like Wallace, although it cost him his life, he changed the United States of America forever. He achieved the impossible dream.

When cynics saw that no man had ever flown through the air before, they accepted that reality. But the idealistic Wright Brothers were different. They dared to dream of a day when we could. They said, *"No, it's true men have never flown before, but why not try? Imagine if we could! How great would that be!"* And so they tried to build the world's first flying contraption. They had no right to believe it was possible because it had never been done before, but they kept believing anyway. After many failures, they too eventually achieved their impossible dream. Today, millions of us fly through the air every year thanks to their pioneering efforts.

It wasn't a cynic who dared to imagine people could communicate in real time across continents through a handheld device in their homes. It was the dreamer, Alexander Graham Bell who said, *"No, people have never had a conversation with each other over hundreds of miles in real time, but what if it was possible? Why not try?"* And so he tried. And he failed. And so he tried some more. And eventually the telephone was born. And now billions of us carry them in our pockets every day.

There's a scene in *Amazing Grace*, the biographical movie that tells the story of Wilberforce's struggle to abolish slavery, where he speaks with his friend, William Pitt. They're both in their early twenties when Pitt reveals he's planning to do something impossible - he wants to become Britain's youngest ever Prime Minister. Pitt explains his plan to Wilberforce who says incredulously, *"William! No one of our age has ever taken power!"* Pitt replies, *"Which is why we're too young to realise that certain things are impossible. Which is why we'll do them anyway."* William Pitt did indeed become Britain's youngest ever Prime Minister soon afterwards, at the age of twenty-four, just like he said he would.

It's always been the ones who are crazy enough to think they can change reality that actually do. Idealists believe in the limitless possibility of their dreams, the beauty of what they'll find, and will dare to imagine and create long after the cynic considers the effort worthless. Therefore, idealism is the root of all progress and the spark of genius. Don't let it go, and all those starry-eyed, crazy fantasies you used to have as a kid are perhaps not as crazy as the world told you they are. Reality can be beaten. You can *change* things.

Young adulthood is the time when we feel this most strongly. Not that we can't feel it at other times in life but our late teens and twenties are almost defined by a feeling that you may recall having at the end of high school or college or university. It's a time where you feel like you're preparing to spread your wings and fly. You're in the Springtime of life. You feel young, healthy and strong - perhaps even invincible - and it's as though all your days have been preparing you for this moment. You've had tastes of freedom and independence already and you're excited about what's ahead. You're ready to explore, to travel, to learn, to fall in love, to get married and to achieve your goals. You see this expectation almost etched on the faces of university graduates as they step out of their commencement ceremonies in particular; full of wide-eyed optimism, they are ready to make their mark on the world. Indeed, their time has come to inherit the earth.

It's this potent blend of youthful vigour and residual optimism that means most of the revolutionary figures of history come from this age bracket. Wilberforce was in his mid twenties when he got started, and in our information age, the revolutionaries would be people like Mark Zuckerberg (Facebook founder), Bill Gates (Microsoft), Steve Jobs (Apple), Elon Musk (Tesla), Larry Page and Sergey Brin (Google). All these guys also got going in their twenties or even teens as they looked to reshape the world and introduce new ideas that no-one had ever thought of.

At this stage in life, whatever is left of their naivety can actually be a strength. Young adults looking to make their mark on the world don't tend to ask "What can be done?" because the truth is that they still don't really know yet. They still have a relatively poor grasp of reality. They haven't worked out the boundaries where the laws of physics or chemistry or human nature go. And it's good that they don't know these things. If they knew about these things, they might not bother trying to go beyond them. It's exactly because they still have a poor grasp of reality that they'll try impossible things. And it's because they'll try impossible things that they'll sometimes succeed, and revolutionise everything we thought we knew.[8]

Instead of asking "What can be done?", young pioneers only ask the question, "What is worth trying to do?" and when they see something worth trying to do, they try to do it. They pursue the vision simply because it's there.

We can all learn something by that. You see, whether we are young or old, if we are embarking on some worthwhile endeavour of our own, we must never ask the question, "Can it be done?" If we ask that question, we are only inviting focus on the obstacles. Whereas, if we ask, "Is this worth trying to do?" we are inviting focus on the possibilities.

Let me illustrate: If Wilberforce had asked, "Can abolishing slavery be done?", he would have heard every member of parliament telling him that it couldn't. He would have seen that no-one had ever done it before. He would have seen that it was far too deeply engrained throughout the British empire to eliminate. He would have seen that it was impossible for one man to change the minds of millions. Therefore, if he'd asked that question, he would have quickly become very cynical and discouraged. He may not have even tried. But he didn't ask that question. He only asked, "Is abolishing slavery worth trying to do?" It was. And so he tried. For fifty years he tried. And eventually he succeeded.

If William Wallace had asked, "can it be done?" regarding the liberation of Scotland, he would have seen the size of the English army and thought not. He would have heard the cynical clan chiefs saying it was impossible. He would have seen the superior English war technology and been intimidated. He would have remembered all the past defeats Scotland had suffered. He would have looked at himself and seen that he was just a commoner who couldn't hope to inspire a whole nation. In short, he would have become discouraged. But he didn't ask that question. He only asked, "Is it worth trying to do?" and the answer was "yes." So he tried. And therefore he succeeded.

If Martin Luther King, the Wright brothers, Alexander Graham Bell or William Pitt had asked "can it be done?" they would have found plentiful reasons to suggest that racial equality, flying through the air, telecommunications and leading a country at twenty-four-years-old were pipe dreams. But they didn't ask that question. They only asked, "Is it worth trying to do?" and the answer was always "yes." So they all tried. And they all succeeded. In doing so, they went beyond the limits of what was previously considered to be possible. It's always this way. Idealists go faster, higher, further and deeper than anyone ever believed.

When Idealism Becomes Faith

We're talking mostly in secular terms so far, but in the Bible, idealism, when allied to confidence in God, becomes known by an even more powerful term. It becomes 'Faith'.

Whereas idealism means attempting great feats without ever knowing if they can be true, faith is a deep conviction that because God is in the great feat, whatever is hoped for has no choice but to become true. Hebrews says, *"Faith is the confidence that what we hope for will actually happen; it gives us assurance about things we cannot see." (Hebrews 11:1)*

The faithful person not only believes in the power of the dream, they believe in the power of the One who *gave* the dream. Where idealism sees Eden and believes; faith sees the One who created Eden and believes all the more. Idealism is powerful but true faith is unstoppable. William Wilberforce actually demonstrated faith rather than idealism, because his hope that slavery could be ended wasn't rooted in his own vision or abilities as much as it was rooted in the power of Jesus Christ. That's why he became an irresistible force for change.

Faith too, never asks, "Can it be done?" Faith always asks, "Is it worth trying to do?" Remember when God asked Moses to lead the Israelites out of slavery in Egypt to the Promised Land? Moses, initially lacked faith and was cynical. He asked, "Can it be done?" and saw all the reasons why it couldn't. He saw that he was too insignificant for mighty Pharaoh to listen to. He saw that he was slow of speech. He saw that Pharaoh was too powerful to be swayed. He saw that his armies were too great to be overcome. He saw that the slavery was too entrenched and Egypt was too dependent on them for Pharaoh to ever consider letting them go. Pessimism threatened to engulf Moses. So God told him to quit asking that question. It was the wrong question. All he needed to ask was, "is it worth trying to do? Is it worth trying to liberate the slaves?" It was. *"So try"*, was God's command. *"Put your trust in me and let me take care of the rest."*

That's faith. Faith is trying the impossible knowing that with God, that word simply has no meaning. And of course, the Bible tells us that when Moses started acting out of faith, he soon *was* doing the impossible. Seas were literally parting in front of him, Pharaoh's armies were being wiped out, and food was falling from the sky. By faith, Israel was being liberated and a new nation was being established.

Remember when Goliath the Philistine was taunting Israel's armies and goading them to send out a challenger to fight him? The cynics in Israel's camp were too fearful to even try. They asked the question, "Can it be done?" and saw plentiful reasons to believe it couldn't. Goliath was so big as to be considered a giant, he was terrifying, he was undefeated...he was undefeatable! But David, to his credit, was the only one who didn't ask that question. David asked by faith, "Is it worth trying to do?" The answer was "yes". So he tried. And God was with him. And soon this little kid, by faith, had taken down a warrior giant with a sling and a stone. He was doing the impossible.

When Peter saw Jesus walking on the waves, he wanted to go out to meet him. Peter could have asked, "can it be done?" and the answer would have been, "no". The laws of Physics say the surface tension of water isn't nearly strong enough to uphold a human being. But Peter didn't ask that question. Instead, he only asked, "is it worth trying to do?" And it was. So by faith, he tried. And by faith, he was soon walking on the water. He was doing the impossible.

When Jesus commissioned the disciples to go preach the gospel, heal the sick, cast out demons and change the world, the disciples could have asked, "can it be done?" and seen nothing but insurmountable obstacles in their path. The Roman Empire, with all its entrenched paganism, was too hostile to Christianity; the pagans would never change their ways; the world was too big to be reached; they were all just working class fishermen and tax collectors. They could have become cynical. But they didn't ask that question. They only asked, "is it worth trying to do?" and the answer was "yes". So by faith, they tried. And God was with them. And by faith they changed the world. By faith, they did the impossible.

Do you see how important it is to ask the right question as a Christian then? Look around you. Turn on the news. What needs to be done right now in your community? What needs to be done in your world? Don't ask whether it can be done; ask only whether it's worth trying to do, and know that by faith, nothing is impossible. As Christians we have been given the same commission as the disciples to preach the gospel, heal the sick, mend the broken-hearted, shine a light in the darkness, love our neighbours, love our enemies, and to bring something of the future kingdom into this world. We are to live a life of transcendent meaning: glorifying God, loving others in practical ways, and bringing wisdom, truth and care into creation. By doing so, we are to show people the way home!

Therefore, genuinely ask yourself right now how you're going to do this. How are you going to glorify God from this day forward? How are you going to love others in a meaningful way from this day forward? How are you going to have a positive impact on creation from this day forward? What would you dream of doing if nothing were holding you back? Do that. It doesn't matter if it seems impossible right now, and God certainly doesn't either. Just do it. Do the impossible.

To be honest, we are failing at this right now. We live in an age where Christians have witnessed the legalisation of abortion, of witchcraft and of homosexual marriage. We've witnessed prayer being banned from schools, we've seen fundamental Christian doctrine outlawed, we've seen free-speech destroyed, and we have lived to become the most persecuted people group in the world. We've increasingly seen heresy and apostasy from those who were meant to be on our side. We've seen an increase in terrorism from the rise of radical Islam. We've seen an escalation of war, disease and natural disasters, and we've seen economic crises threatening to engulf the whole planet. We've seen poverty and corruption near and far, and we've seen migration crises threatening to destabilise society. We've seen many animal species become endangered or extinct on our watch and we've seen ignorance rather than wisdom beginning to darken the minds of men.

Our failure has not so much been that all this has happened on our watch, but rather in the fact we have largely become so cynical about what can be done in response, that we have largely given up and decided to do nothing. We look at the TV screens and we complain to each other, shake our heads and then ultimately just shrug and say, "Well this is just the way the world is!" This is not the response God wants from us. He doesn't want that kind of cynicism.

Can we change things? Who knows...maybe not. But that's not even the right question! The question faith asks is, "what is worth trying to do?" Is it worth *trying* to give people the gospel, heal the sick, care for the broken-hearted, establish the truth, oppose immorality, defend the weak, shine a light in the darkness, and speak out for righteousness? It is. It will always be worth trying to do those things. So let's try. Let's try that. Let's rage against the dying of the light and give our lives for the worthiest of causes knowing that by faith, anything is possible. The only failure in God's kingdom, as in life, is not to try. It's to let fear stop you from even stepping outside the front door.

And do you know what, I bet you *won't* fail. I bet you'll do the impossible. What do the stories of Moses, David, Peter and the disciples exist in our Bibles for if not to tell us that we can be just like them. Jesus said, *"I tell you the truth, anyone who believes in me will do the same works I have done, and even greater works, because I am going to be with the Father."* (John 14:12) We just need *faith!* So again, look around. What needs to be done? Whatever it is, do it. Do it now. Do great things. Do difficult things. Do worthwhile things. Do impossible things. Remember, by faith God's people have parted seas, established nations, brought down city walls, overthrown kingdoms, ruled with justice, shut the mouths of lions, quenched the flames of fire, put whole armies to flight and raised the dead. You can do likewise. You can do the impossible. Just try.

God Has Work For You To Do

God has work for all of us to do. Paul writes, *"For we are God's masterpiece. He has created us anew in Christ Jesus, so we can do the good things he planned for us long ago."* (Ephesians 2:10) Many of us already know what that work is. And many of us have already acted upon the call on our lives.

I heard recently about an American girl called Katie Davis, who felt called from an early age to go to Uganda as a missionary. Therefore, immediately after finishing high school, she flew off to Africa to get started. By the age of nineteen, she had adopted ten girls there (now fourteen girls), and established an entire new ministry primarily aimed at educating children.

As the ministry grew, she was eventually able to build a high school and then she expanded into helping women out of the sex trade by offering them the chance to make money through jewellery making. She began changing reality and making it look a tiny bit more like heaven for those Ugandans.

The whole thing wasn't without opposition. And if Katie Davis had asked the question, "Can it be done?" the likelihood is she would never have gone. It was dangerous. She was young. She was getting involved with troubled lives and she had no previous experience of this kind of work. But Katie only asked, "Is it worth trying to do?" and she saw that it was. Furthermore, she knew God had called her to it, and so she went. Indeed, I understand that she is still there changing lives to this day.[9]

I wish I had been as immediately faithful as Katie. I felt called to start The Fuel Project ministry in my early twenties but to be honest, the vision looked much bigger than anything I had a right to believe in. Writing books; making video series and films; connecting Christians around the world; Christian art exhibitions; debates; music shows; evangelism; clothing; smartphone apps...that was the ideal. But to my discredit, when I asked if it could be done, I thought the answer was "no". Like Moses, I saw too many obstacles. I thought I was too young. I thought that because no-one knew who I was, nobody would listen. I thought that I didn't have enough money or resources to start a ministry. I thought that I wouldn't be able to eat or put a roof over my head that way. So I actually delayed launching The Fuel Project for many years.

Instead I started a property management company to generate an income. This was my way of participating in The

System on flexible terms. The idea was that one day when it was established, I'd employ managers to take care of it and only then would I fully be able to turn my attention to The Fuel Project.

Property management wasn't particularly fulfilling for me or even very successful. Just as things were starting to come together in the fourth year an economic crash unravelled most of the good work that had been done until that point. And that period led to be the darkest time of my life. The fact is that as I was entering into my late twenties, I was not yet generating enough money for full financial independence and as I was watching as my peers became successful in The System, getting jobs and promotions, earning enough for homes and cars, getting married, having kids and going on nice vacations, I began to feel like a complete failure. Comparison after all, is so often the root of misery.

The worst moment was perhaps at one of my old school friends' wedding. I didn't have a girlfriend to go with and I hadn't been able to afford a decent suit, so I went looking a bit scruffy and alone. All my old friends there had wives and new babies, and the conversation was filled with news of their job promotions, house purchases, vacations and recent activities.

As they danced with their partners that evening, I sat alone at a table in the corner, and endured occasional jibes about my scruffy appearance. And I realised then that I had never felt like such a failure. It made me wish so much that I could throw in the towel on the path I was pursuing. I hated that my idealism had got me chasing silly, unrealistic, impossible fantasies about starting a ministry, and I hated that I couldn't give those fantasies up. Because no matter how dark a hole I was in, and no matter how bad I felt, the idea of throwing in the towel; of giving up on the ministry dream, filled me with a dread that I can't even describe. It felt like I'd be giving up on life itself. Earl Denman wrote, *"I grew up with an ambition and determination without which I would have been a good deal happier. I thought a lot and developed the faraway look of a dreamer, for it was always the distant heights that fascinated me and drew me to them in spirit. I was not sure what could be accomplished with tenacity and little else, but the target was high and each rebuff only saw me more determined to see at least one major dream to its fulfilment."*[10]

Like Denman, I felt that if I'd not been so idealistic, I could have been a good deal happier. Becoming cynical would have been so much *easier*. After all, pursuing the dream had led nowhere. I had achieved nothing, neither in property management or in the ministry. And the stark facts were that I had little money, no house of my own, no wife, no kids, no girlfriend, no prospects, hadn't had a holiday in years, was ashamed, increasingly depressed, isolated and losing self-esteem.

During this time I would shout to God for help. I'd cry. I'd pray for hours. At the start of every year I'd fast for forty days straight in sheer desperation. I'd argue with God and ask him why he was calling me in the direction of this ministry when it led nowhere. And then when I was at my lowest ebb, with nothing left to lose...I realised that God had never asked me to start a property management company in the first place!

You see, the property management company had come out of my lack of faith - out of my fear and cynicism. I wasn't pursuing the dream at all! I'd started managing because when

God had told me to start a ministry, I'd asked "Can it be done?" and concluded that it couldn't. I'd thought The System was too large an obstacle and that I'd need to deal with it somehow first. Therefore, I'd gotten off track and become distracted with rent agreements and insurance forms - that was my daily life, and God hadn't asked me to do any of it. He'd asked me to start a ministry. That's all.

Everything changed for me when I stopped looking at the obstacles to The Fuel Project and instead asked, "Is it worth trying to do?" I knew that it was. And that's all that mattered. How would I put a roof over my head and eat while running a ministry? I still had no idea. Not a single clue. But since I wasn't exactly achieving that through property management anyway, I really had nothing to lose. I decided in that moment, really for the first time, to literally jump in with both feet and follow the dream.

By faith, and nothing else, I began writing *Know Your Enemy* for The Fuel Project on an obsolete laptop. I made videos on a budget of exactly £0 using free software and microphone, and started releasing them all for free on YouTube. By faith, I did what God asked and trusted him to do the rest. And he did. Somehow I was able to go full-time with the ministry just a couple of years later. And the church network is now up and running. And this is now the sixth title to be released under the Fuel name. And literally hundreds of people have now written to say they came to Christ through the ministry.

For the first time, I'm truly living out the threefold meaning of life, loving God, telling others about him, and pursuing a worthy cause. And impossible things have happened as a result. Like Katie Davis and so many others out there, there's still much more of the vision to pursue and I don't want to get complacent because I'm sure there are many more challenges ahead, but the journey until now has been so fun. And right now I feel like when it's time for me to go home, I'll be content.

I speak from experience when I say this then: If God has given you a dream to pursue, then you must begin it right away. In fact, this is the best piece of advice I can now give: Begin. Just get started. Forget about what you lack, what you might need in the future, what the obstacles are, and all the rest. Don't make the mistake I made. Simply begin. Begin today. Begin wherever you are. Begin with fear. Begin with doubt. Begin with hands shaking. Begin with voice trembling. Begin with whatever you have. But just begin. God will take care of the rest. You can trust him. You really can. Put yourself in his hands, have the boldness to take concrete steps in the direction of your goals, and you'll soon find there's a power in it beyond your own.

Don't make my mistake in thinking you're pursuing the dream, when you're really not, either. Are you really living from faith right now or are your actions secretly driven by fear and cynicism? You don't need to come at the dream God's given you from a side angle like I did. Just go straight at it and let Him clear your way.

It won't be easy, don't be under any miscomprehensions about this. Remember it took Wilberforce fifty years to achieve the abolition of the slave trade. Reality is not effortlessly changed. And if you're pursuing a mission given by God, Satan and his demons will come at you with every weapon in their armoury. Indeed, Satan knows that his best plan of attack against you is to cause you to lose heart. So expect it.

But don't let it happen. Whenever you're feeling a little bit beaten up, take your stand. *"Be strong in the Lord and in his mighty power...put on every piece of God's armour so that you will be able to resist the enemy in the time of evil. Then after the battle you will still be standing firm. Stand your ground, putting on the belt of truth and the body armour of God's righteousness. For shoes, put on the peace that comes from the Good News so that you will be fully prepared. In addition to all of these, hold up the shield of faith to stop the fiery arrows of the devil." (Ephesians 6:10,13-16)* Notice what repels Satan's attacks? Faith. Keep your faith alive and it shields you from discouragement and cynicism. And I want to emphasise that if you're to succeed in your purpose, it really is going to take more courage than you think you've got. You're going to need the heart of a lion.

I guess finally for this section, if God has given you a vocation to pursue, know that it won't always fit in a box and it won't always make sense, even to the people around you. Katie Davis' parents really didn't understand her desire to go to Uganda and were initially against the idea. There were times when my path worried my parents and baffled my friends too. God sometimes tells us to do things that don't really make obvious sense. Whether it be David taking on Goliath with a sling and a stone, Moses going to Pharaoh to demand the release of the slaves, Peter walking on water, or a ragtag group of fishermen being sent out to change the world, God is a specialist at turning accepted wisdom on its head.

Live With Purpose Wherever You Are

Of course, God may not be calling you to go to Uganda or start a full-time ministry. I may be at risk of being misunderstood here so I must take a moment to clarify. Living a meaningful life for God doesn't necessarily mean coming out of The System and going to live in an African mud-hut. It doesn't necessarily mean starting a full-time ministry either. In fact, living a meaningful life for God might mean staying exactly where you are. What I mean is, God may call you to be an accountant, a hairdresser or a bank manager.

If a meaningful life is to love God, love others, and to spend it in a worthy cause, then Jesus combined all three when he gave us the Great Commission: *"Therefore go and make disciples of all the nations, baptising them in the name of the Father and the Son and the Holy Spirit. Teach these new disciples to obey all the commands I have given you. And be sure of this: I am with you always, even to the end of the age."* (Matthew 28:19-20) Jesus tells us to go into the places where corruption, darkness, ignorance and pain reigns, and to redeem it somehow from within. To bring light and healing with us. To be in the world, but not of it.

It's actually strange that Christians have often struggled with this concept. We've often got it into our heads that being a Christian means total withdrawal from the world. Monks and nuns, for example, who claim to be dedicating their lives to Jesus, hole themselves up in isolated monasteries and nunneries as a sign of their extreme devotion, where they can't possibly hope to influence the world in any tangible way. Wouldn't it be a more extreme act of devotion to actually do what the Lord commanded? To actively go *into* the world to make disciples, rather than withdrawing from it? But Evangelical Christians too, will often define their faith only by what they do when they are isolated from the world, in church buildings on Sunday mornings. Some will even isolate themselves from unbelievers throughout the week. This is puzzling because Jesus has never asked for physical separation from the world. Again, Jesus has told us to go *into* the world - *into* the places of brokenness especially - and to preach, heal and restore. *That's* what actually defines our faith.

Jesus in fact, modelled this himself through his incarnation. When he saw the world was corrupted under the power of sin, he didn't isolate himself from it. Instead, he came down from his lofty position and entered into the world to redeem it from within. He got in amongst the filth and brokenness and preached, healed and restored.

That's our remit. And since we all know The System is broken, corrupted, and full of men and women who don't know Christ, it shouldn't surprise us if Jesus wants some of us to be there. Therefore, if you are a car salesman, a factory worker, a teacher, a scientist, an accountant, a fireman, a bank manager, an engineer, a store assistant, or something else, don't think that you need to come out of those jobs to live a meaningful life. Quite the opposite. Paul wrote that unless otherwise instructed, *"each of you should remain as you were when God called you. Are you a slave? Don't let that worry you - but if you get a chance to be free, take it." (1 Corinthians 7:20-21)* We are to be Jesus' hands and feet wherever we are: In the car showroom, in the factory, in the classroom, in the laboratory, in the office, in the fire station, at the bank, on the oil rig, in the store, or anywhere else. Paul's saying that even if you were a *slave*, you could fulfil the threefold meaning of life to glorify God, love others and care for creation right where you are.

Again, I know that many of us get tired with The System and the troubles of the world, so finding a cabin in the woods, living off-grid, eating homegrown vegetables and catching our own meals seems rather appealing at times, but as a Christian, how much impact would you really have on the world if you retreated from it? Isn't it better you stay where you are, if it means you can redeem your immediate neighbourhood in some way? You'll have plenty of time to rest when you get home, but that's not what this world is all about. The moment The Fall happened, there was a recovery mission to get involved with. Jesus asks us to play a role in it as his hands and feet. Therefore, here on this earth, we have work to do.

William Wilberforce is a great example again. When he first converted to Christianity, he briefly considered withdrawing from The System. He wanted to quit his role in politics, withdraw from public life altogether, and enter into a life of contemplation and solitude. However, after speaking with friends, especially John Newton, the composer of *Amazing Grace*, and thinking it over for himself, he thankfully realised that the Lord hasn't asked that of us. Instead, Wilberforce remained in The System as a politician, and used that position for the kingdom. He worked through politics to glorify God, end slavery, improve morality and make a better life for animals, amongst other things. He lived a meaningful life where he was.

Let's do the same. If we all take our lights away from the workplace, the university campus or the school and retreat to some distant enclave, those places we leave behind will only get darker. Stay where God called you and redeem it from within. Change realities that way. (Incidentally, this is also why Christian alternatives for Facebook and YouTube are misguided. Don't withdraw from social media on these grounds. Instead, bring redemption from within.)

I was mistaken as a teenager to believe that all the commuters on my school bus were broken simply because they were in The System. Being in The System wasn't the problem. It was the fact that they had no other transcendent cause outwith The System that was the problem. But if you're a Christian, you go into The System and take the transcendent cause with you. Your workplace becomes a mission field. The office becomes an opportunity to reveal something of the future kingdom. The darkness of your staffroom becomes a chance to be a light that shows the way home. You live a life of meaning through wherever God has called you to be.

What if you don't feel called by God to be in any particular job at all? Then begin doing meaningful things with your spare time. The trick here is to ask yourself what your gifts are. What makes you come alive? What do you love to do the most? Sing? Dance? Cook? Play sports? Knit? Eat? Run? Photography? What you *desire* to do; what you're passionate about, normally reveals what God *designed* you to do. To make it meaningful, you simply have to use your gift and passion to glorify God, love others, and care for creation in some way. At that point, it ceases to become just a past-time and instead becomes a part of your threefold purpose.

For example, if you love to play music, then can you get a band together, write God glorifying songs, and sing in local coffee shops? If so, a past-time has just become a purpose. Do you love food? Then can you start doing summer BBQ outreach events in your community to develop relationships with neighbours? If so, a past-time has just become a purpose. Do you love to run? Then can you organise a Christian running club and wear t-shirts with John 3:16 on the back to witness to the public as you go? Do you love to knit? Then can you knit warm hats and gloves to give to the homeless? Do you love to bake? Then can you bake freebies to hand out to the homeless on the street, or even just to neighbours with a little tract and a whole lot of love attached? If so, past-times have just become purposes.

It's just about being intentional. As you look around at the circumstances of your neighbours, your community and your world, ask what's worth trying to do, and then find a way to do it with your gifting. There are literally millions of ways you can do this. Be creative and be passionate.

Whose Cause Is Best?

Let's not argue amongst ourselves about whose cause is best either. In 2015, there was an uproar on social media because a famous and beloved lion in Zimbabwe called Cecil, had been killed by an American trophy hunter. Lion numbers are drastically low already and this loss of life was rightly seen as a sickening work of vanity.

Not long afterwards, a different scandal hit the news where it turned out the Planned Parenthood organisation in the United States had been harvesting parts from aborted babies and selling them for profit. Of course, this was another sickening example of just how debauched our world is becoming.

What was interesting was the way that Christians argued amongst themselves over which of these issues was most important. Some Christians expressed their dismay about Cecil the Lion and were roundly chastised for it. They were told, "You people getting worked up about a lion! It's just a lion! If only you got as animated about human babies being aborted and having their parts harvested as you do about lions, then we might get somewhere in life!" Arguments raged about what was worth getting animated about and what wasn't and each side chastised the other for not giving more support to their cause.

It was all rather unnecessary. If someone devotes their life to animal conservation; if that's what moves them; are they not fulfilling the threefold meaning of life in their own way? Wasn't wise care of creation and the creatures that God made, part of our remit in Genesis? Of course it was. If people are passionate about animal conservation then they should stay passionate and do what they can in that field. Similarly, if someone devotes their life to ending abortion and the abhorrent practice of selling body parts because that's what moves them, are they not fulfilling the threefold meaning of life too? Of course they are. So let them be passionate and do what they can also.

Why should one preclude the other? Let's all work to fulfil the threefold meaning according to our own gifts and passions and in our own way. God has made us all unique, to be different parts of one body. One part shouldn't say to the other that it's more important. It simply does what it was made to do. And if it makes the world a better, more God-honouring place to live in some way, a good job has been done. Therefore, instead of discouraging each other, or arguing about who's doing the real work of the kingdom, let's all encourage and support *any* work for the kingdom.

So again, if your passion is for animals, then become a vet or get involved in conservation. If your passion is for the marginalised, then get involved with work for addicts and the homeless. If your passion is for the disabled, work to improve their condition. If your gift is for cinematography, then make films for the kingdom. And let's not bicker or wonder whether what we're doing is as important as what someone else is doing. Let's just do what we can, where we are, with what we have.

Again, I'm no longer even talking about careers here either. Regardless of what you do to earn money, work towards some kind of meaningful goal in your life. Even if it feels small. Who's to say that knitting some homeless guys some hats in your spare time won't mean as much to the kingdom in the end as a full-time missionary's work? Who's to say your two mites won't have as much impact as someone else's 'millions'? Little is much when God is in it. So just do something, and do it in Jesus' name.

Discouragement

All I'm really trying to do here is to encourage you to go toe-to-toe with life. That feeling of optimism and hope you had as a young adult? There's a truth in that. We should come here to take the whole fallen thing on and put up a good fight. If possible, give it a good thrashing. The best kind of thrashing, mind you. Change it. Mould it. Shape it. Take broken things and fix them. Go to dark places and shine lights. Take bad things and make them better. Bring something of home to earth right now. I know how insanely difficult it will be. I'm aware of the discouragement you're going to face. And I know you're going to want to quit, but don't lose heart. Please don't. People need you. You're an ambassador.

Don't listen to the cynics. Imagine as the Wright Brothers stood beside the wreckage of yet another mangled plane wreckage how the onlookers would have sneered: *"Still trying to fly eh, boys? What do you think you are, ducks? You're certainly quackers! You're crazy! It's time to give up on these pie-in-the-sky schemes and start living in the real world! Whoever heard of such a barmy idea as flying humans! It's never been done! It can't be done! Give it up!"*

People who have given up on their own dreams will always find a way to discourage you from yours. And if you're attempting anything for God, expect it all the more. David was laughed at when he stepped out to face Goliath. The soldiers on Jericho's walls laughed in bemusement at Joshua and the Israelites as they marched round the city. Noah was mocked while building the ark. Jesus was mocked as he went to the cross.

Perhaps you've already experienced this. People telling you that you're not smart enough, strong enough, brave enough, talented enough or skilled enough to pursue the dream God has put in your heart. But don't listen. God consistently uses the weak and despised things of this world to change reality because it's through them that his power and glory is most vividly seen. (William Wilberforce was only 5'3" by the way!) So God can use you too.

Idealism, and indeed its stronger cousin, Faith, is only ever praised in hindsight. Once success has been achieved, idealists go down in history as visionaries. Pioneers. Revolutionaries. Heroes. People who created a better world. Stories will be told of them, and their determination and resilience in the darkest hours will be marvelled at. People will weep and applaud and their lives will be held up as an example for all future generations. Books and movies will be written about them and they'll win Oscars. But don't expect any of that at the start. Before success has been achieved, idealists are merely known as loonies. Childish fantasists. Corny, pitiable, simple-minded, unsophisticated, naive fools who can't get their head out of the clouds and who aren't living in the real world. In those days it may just be you and Jesus against the world. But believe me, that's a winning team. And God's foolishness is wiser than man's wisdom.

So one final time, never ask "Can it be done?" Only ask "Is it worth trying to do?" If it's worth trying to do, then try to do it, and never stop trying to do it. No matter what anyone says. Try to surround yourself with people who will support you. But never give up. Never, ever, ever give up. Better is a life spent pursuing an impossible dream than one spent refusing to even try. And remember that cynicism isn't wisdom; it's brokenness. It's defeat. Keep getting up. Keep going. Reality can be beaten. You can do this.

I'll finish by saying that there are some pursuits where success isn't even the point. Sometimes it's the journey rather than the destination that matters. I mean, even if Wilberforce had never lived to see slavery abolished, would he have chosen to live any other way? I don't think so. The point is that he'd still have lived a life of meaning. He'd still have tried. And that would have been the real glory. What else would he rather have spent his life for? There are some transcendent pursuits where, win or lose, you'll know you've been alive, and you'll finish life a contented and peaceful soul, whatever the outcome. Furthermore, the world will likely have been better for your living in it. It's like the famous song, *The Impossible Dream*:

To dream the impossible dream
To fight the unbeatable foe
To bear the unbearable sorrow
To run where the brave dare not go

To right the unrightable wrong
To love pure and chaste from afar
To try when your arms are too weary
To reach the unreachable star

This is my quest, to follow that star
No matter how hopeless, no matter how far
To fight without question or pause
To be willing to march into hell for a heavenly cause

And I know if I'll only be true to this glorious quest

That my heart will lie peaceful and calm when I'm laid to my
rest

And the world will be better for this
That one man, scorned and covered with scars
Still strove with his last ounce of courage
To reach the unreachable star.[11]

Let's all live like that. And if that sounds too corny to you and you don't think it can be done, then please get out of the way of those who are doing it. You may just thank them for it later. They may just be changing the world.

Chapter Six

Adulthood

"The ability to retain a child's view of the world with at the same time a mature understanding of what it means to retain it, is extremely rare - and a person who has these qualities is likely to be able to contribute something really important to our thinking." - Mortimer J. Adler

---

If you're reading this while you're young, I can't tell you exactly when you'll begin to feel like a proper adult. In fact, I can't guarantee you'll ever feel like an adult at all. It's a strange thing but when you're a child you look up to them and suspect they have life all figured out. You think that one day you'll wake up and you'll have it all figured out too, and you'll just feel...adultish. Like a caterpillar turning into a butterfly, you are now one sort of thing, but there will come an age when you'll transform into another sort of thing and everything will instantly look and feel completely different.

On that day, you'll know the answer to everything. You'll know, for example, why cows sleep standing up, why crabs don't have eyebrows, how hard you would have to jump to never come back down, why some people are left-handed, why flies think gross stuff smells nice, and whether a shaved baby gorilla would look like a really ugly baby or just a gorilla. You'll suddenly be able to throw as far as you like, and breathe underwater, and if you really wanted to, you could make a spaceship. Because you're a super adult.

It doesn't work like that though. There tends not to be a specific moment when you stop being one thing and begin being another. You see, even though your body is getting older, and yes, hopefully you're acquiring wisdom along the way, there's an inner part of you that somehow always feels the same age. Therefore, discovering that you're an adult can actually come as a bit of a shock. I remember the first time I bought my own toilet roll and the startling thought went through my head that I may have passed into adulthood without realising. I mean, this was surely only a thing that adults would do? And yet I still didn't really feel like one inside.

In fact, for a long time, I felt like I was only pretending to be an adult. I kept hoping that someday soon I would wake up and feel fully mature and in control of life, but in the meantime I was always worried my facade would slip and everyone would discover the truth that I was just faking it. I remember sitting down for meetings with property management clients, wearing a suit and talking about very serious contracts, and worrying the whole thing would come to a screeching halt when it slipped out that I still drank the milk from the bottom of my cereal bowl, and that en-route to the meeting I'd been singing along to *The Pirates Who Don't Do Anything* from Veggie Tales in the car. There was a certain sense in which I felt like I was playing dress-up by wearing that suit and that I was sure to be found out as an impostor.

I think the moment I knew something had changed forever though, was when my dad died. Up until that moment, everything in my universe had been set in its course. Even though all my grandparents had died in my teens, my great aunt and great uncle kept representing that generation in my family for a long time afterwards. My parents, aunts and uncles then represented the next generation down. And while both those generations existed, myself, siblings and cousins were always, at least in relation to them, 'the kids'. We were regarded as the kids even when we were in our mid twenties. We each still had to find love, settle down, have kids of our own and create our own lives, so even at that time, life always felt like something that was up ahead for us. It was something we were working towards and preparing for, like some distant mountain peak that we would scale one day when the time was right.

In the meantime, allowances were still made for us on account of our youth and we never had to occupy the areas of ultimate responsibility. At family events for example, the cooking of meals was always undertaken by the older women and the pre-meal prayers of thanksgiving were down to the older men. Although our upbringing had taught us it was courteous to offer to help, we'd often be turned away and told simply to relax.

Around the age of thirty however, both my great aunt and uncle died in quick succession, and then my dad too. I can't really explain what kind of impact that had in words, but I just knew that everything had indeed changed. I suddenly realised that life was no longer something that was up ahead for me; I was in it. This was it. This was adulthood. Maybe I still didn't feel like an adult even now; maybe I never would, but nonetheless, here I was. Perhaps for you, everything changed when you got married and suddenly realised you had another person in your life to take care of, serve and protect. Perhaps it was when you moved into your first home and realised that if you didn't pay the rent or mortgage, no-one else would. Perhaps it was when you had your first baby and felt the full weight of responsibility that comes with a little life that was completely and utterly dependent on you. Whenever it was, the key component of becoming an adult was almost certainly the moment that you first felt *responsible.* That's really the essence of adulthood: responsibility. It's when you become responsible for buying your own toilet paper, cooking your own food, paying your own bills, saying the pre-meal prayers at family gatherings, facing the troubles and trials of life independently, taking responsibility for others too, and when you are eventually doing all of this in the knowledge that the buck now stops entirely with you.

Responsibility can be a scary thing, and in an increasingly tumultuous and frightening world, there is an epidemic of people who are desperate to avoid it. However, if your parents did a good job when you were growing up, when they began retracting the wall of protection around you in your teens, they'll have also begun letting you shoulder the responsibility for your own actions. Therefore, you'll have been slowly growing into this moment for some time.

Gradually, you'll have been learning to make your own decisions, take responsibility for the consequences of those decisions, carry your own burdens, and indeed roll with life's punches. You may have already made some huge mistakes and learned some hard lessons, but you'll have learned how to pick yourself up and keep going, and from here on in, as we now know, that's really what life's all about. Taking the blows and keep moving forward. Facing disappointments and pain without becoming cynical and without losing faith. That's how winning is done.

But I'm afraid that no-one gets this far into the fight completely unbruised. By the time you hit thirty, you *will* have now lost people close to you through death; you *will* have experienced a great deal of personal suffering and disappointment; you *will* have quite possibly taken a job in The System in which you find no meaning or pleasure, and your spirit may, through the passing of the years, have been somewhat worn down, if not yet entirely crushed by the monotonous grind. Furthermore, you will have seen much more of corruption, terrorism, disaster and death than you ever cared to see, and you may have been on the verge of throwing your hands up in despair many times as you encountered the devastating combination of life's big right hooks and small left jabs. As a result of all your experiences until now, you will now almost certainly be carrying some emotional wounds, and therefore scabs.

Furthermore, as a result of all this, you may now have developed some coping mechanisms to manage the pain.

Coping Mechanisms/Pain Management

While I was in my late teens and early twenties and going through university, I also worked part-time at Costco Wholesale. Since I'd known many of my workmates there from childhood, we would often do things together when we had spare time. For example, we would play football together; in Winter we'd go snowboarding; and in Summer we'd plan to go rafting on the river.

As time went on however, I found my friends increasingly wanted to involve alcohol in all these activities. Playing football was no longer enough fun by itself-they wanted to take a bottle of vodka and turn it into a drinking game. Snowboarding was no longer enough-they wanted to be drunk before they hit the slopes. River rafting on a summer's day wasn't enough either-they wanted to take a case of beers to guzzle along the way. The experiences themselves gradually seemed to be losing their appeal. Increasingly, the only activity that had any real attraction for them was getting inebriated.

I remember feeling confused and wistful about this. I wondered what had happened to the innocent days of childhood when we actually found pure joy in simple pleasures. When playing football from dawn to dusk was enough; when sledging in the snow, swinging from trees, running through sprinklers, rafting down rivers and jumping in Autumn leaves was enough. When we loved the vibrancy and vitality of life so much, and when it all seemed so wondrous, that numbing ourselves to it with alcohol didn't hold any appeal. It's only as I got older that I could make sense of what was happening-I realised that the increasing dependence on alcohol amongst my friends was merely a sign that they were losing heart.

Alcohol numbs the senses, you see. It takes the hard edge off life and dampens our ability to feel. That's what we often want as adults. When we grow up and discover how reality hurts in surprising and cruel ways, we naturally want to be anesthetised from it somehow. And that's what alcohol does. It's an anaesthetic for life. It's a type of self-medication. A coping mechanism. People drink when they're sad, frustrated, depressed, dissatisfied, angry, feeling hopeless, or reeling in pain, simply because they just don't want to feel quite so intensely anymore.

I'm going to pin at least some of this on The System again. The System as we know it in the West, can be traced back to the British Industrial Revolution of the 18th to 19th Centuries. For all the wonderful progress that the revolution brought, it was effectively the beginning of a new type of wage labour. Instead of working to provide food and shelter for one's own family and immediate neighbourhood through farming, crofting and cottage industry as in centuries past, huge factories and smoking mills were now erected and the 9-5 working day (i.e. the forty hour week) was eventually established for the common man. Initially people actually were forced to work much longer hours than that, but over time, a compromise was reached where they at least were allowed to keep evenings and weekends free. Even so, this is when humans first had the potential to feel like meaningless cogs in a large industrial machine.

Statistics show how inner-city alcoholism spiked in Great Britain around this time (as we noted earlier when referring to Wilberforce's mission) and it's explained in part by the fact that life became such miserable, monotonous drudgery for these industrial wage labourers, that they began using alcohol as a kind of escape. Sitting in pubs on the way home from work at 5pm, drinking themselves into oblivion, became a way of grabbing a holiday from everything their lives had become - rent, debt and seemingly endless hard labour. Indeed, they often drank to stupefy themselves so much that all the money they had just made that day in the factory would get blown immediately at the bar. And of course, violence, riots and other expressions of frustration were soon to follow. People are never so frustrated with others as when they're frustrated with themselves.

Not much has really changed since then. Many people are still doing jobs they hate from 9-5 each day, still feeling like faceless cogs in a machine, still feeling like the treadmill they're on is endless and futile, and therefore still turning to alcohol in exactly the same way to numb their pain. Many are still basically living for the weekends when they get to frequent bars or clubs, getting utterly inebriated to forget about everything their lives have become. Sometimes in frustration, they're still taking it out on others by brawling in the streets. And even on a more civilised and refined level, many people still regard the highlight of their day as the moment they get home from work and pour themselves a large glass or wine...or two...or three...to help them 'unwind' or 'de-stress' from everything they've just experienced. Furthermore, it takes their minds off the fact it's already getting dark, and they're due to do it all again tomorrow.

The lure of alcohol then, even today, remains centred on the fact that it dampens our ability to feel. And indeed, for many then, life without alcohol would make living seem virtually unbearable. They *need* this coping mechanism. It becomes an obsession. An idol. It occupies a position in their lives that no mere liquid should ever have a right to. Therefore, when you get to the modern statistics about alcohol abuse, what we're largely reading about is the extent of society's pain. Here are some of those stats:

- In England, around 18% of the population are thought to be drinking damagingly high quantities of alcohol. Nearly a fifth.[1]
- In England, alcohol-related deaths have risen by 19% in the past 10 years.[1]
- In Europe, around 23 million people are estimated to be dependent on alcohol.[2]
- In Europe, alcohol contributes towards nearly 1 in 10 of all cases of illness and premature deaths.[2]
- In the United States, alcohol abuse is the third highest cause of death, claiming 88,000 each year.[3]
- In the United States, alcohol excess costs the economy $223.5 billion per year.[3]

The catch-22 of alcohol is that it's a depressant. Therefore, drinking it in excess is likely to make an individual *more* depressed in the long-run. Although it momentarily numbs the pain, it essentially makes it worse when the effects wear off and they can feel again. And this is often the downward spiral that leads to alcoholism. Feel bad, numb it, feel worse, numb it some more.

Drug abuse is another method by which people try to escape reality. We won't go into the figures for drugs - needless to say drug abuse isn't quite as widespread as alcohol abuse - but the stats are as shocking as those for alcohol in their own way, and the reason for their proliferation is the same: they simply help the user forget about reality. The famous writer, Edgar Allen

Poe, once said, *"I have absolutely no pleasure in the stimulants in which I sometimes so madly indulge. It has not been the pursuit of pleasure that I have periled life and reputation and reason. It has been the desperate attempt to escape torturing memories, from a sense of insupportable loneliness and a dread of some strange impending doom."*[4]

This is really very insightful and honest. Consciously, people may believe they are drinking and taking recreational drugs because it's fun or pleasurable, but the real psychology behind it is escapism. You see, in adulthood, we're often more lonely, upset, disappointed, dissatisfied or depressed than we even realise. And because we've been living with these feelings for so long, we can't remember life being any other way. We can't remember what it was like when we didn't feel at least a little bit tired or burdened or worried. It's only our outward coping mechanisms that betray the pain that's really in our hearts. They show that we're subconsciously looking for anaesthetics, and when the anaesthetics relieve the sadness for just a moment, the relief is interpreted by us to be pleasure.

Poe again wrote tellingly on the subject when he said, *"I became insane, with long intervals of horrible sanity."*[5] It was the sanity he found hard to bear and it was the insanity when he felt free. Drunkenness and drug trips are a deliberate attempt to induce a kind of liberating insanity. They're an attempt to escape reality.

Promiscuous sex is another form of pain management. It isn't really the pursuit of pleasure that primarily causes men to use prostitutes. What really drives them is loneliness, and a despairing lack of love and true intimacy. Brief encounters with random women mask their pain for a while and help them cope with another day. Behind the use of pornography is the same idea. Even virtual sex with a screen can liberate them from the pain for a while and offer some kind of relief. Men and women jumping into bed with a new partner every week isn't a sign of health and stability in their hearts - it's a sign that these people are craving intimacy but are too hurt, bitter, cynical, broken and jaded to enter into a committed, selfless, responsible relationships that will require them to trust and be vulnerable with each other. They are simply using sex for pain management.

And have you noticed that adulthood has now almost come to be *defined* by these coping mechanisms? Have you noticed for example that the word 'Adult', which formerly simply referred simply to the age of responsibility, has now come to be a byword for sex, drugs, alcohol abuse and other forms of depravity?

For example, if someone asked you to go see an 'Adult Movie' with them, you would expect to see sexually explicit content, and possibly a lot more besides. If you were to hear that a new 'Adult Store' was opening up in town, you would know it's probably going to stock all kinds of sexual paraphernalia designed to cater to every fetish. If you're watching television and a show is introduced with a warning that it contains 'Adult Themes', you'd know that if you keep watching you are going to witness anything from incest to rape, from murder to gore, from drug abuse to torture. Indeed, put the word 'Adult' in front of anything and it's a euphemistic descriptor for strong, if not horrific content. We define 'adulthood' now by how knowing we are of the sin that pervades the world, *and* by the kind of coping mechanisms we use to survive it.

I find all this so tragic, and I find it even more sad when bitter, resentful adults become nihilistic with their pain. We spoke earlier about how teenagers turn to nihilism to express their hopelessness. But adults do it too.

There was a movie released some years ago by Seth MacFarlane, called "Ted". The premise is that a young kid called John Bennett (played by Mark Wahlberg) makes a childhood wish for his teddy bear to come to life. His wish comes true, but as they both grow up into adulthood, Ted, like John, becomes a drug taking, prostitute-cavorting, hard-drinking, brawling, potty-mouthed cynic. People obviously loved it because a sequel was made a couple of years later. But the humour simply comes from the shock factor of innocence being subverted and naivety being warped.

It's sad when we take pleasure in the corruption of innocence like that. You find it in YouTube videos where people have dubbed curse words into the middle of children's TV shows. You find it on the internet where people have drawn cartoon characters from their childhood in sexual poses or taking drugs. This 'humour' is actually the cry of those who, having lost their own innocence, have corruption now spilling out of them. It's like they have come to hate innocence for it having been a lie and deliberately find a twisted pleasure in destroying it for others too.

At any rate, Peter warned against all these destructive coping mechanisms and more when he said, *"Dear friends, I warn you as 'temporary residents and foreigners' to keep away from worldly desires that wage war against your very souls." (1*

143

Peter 2:11) Peter is reminding us that we're only passing through this world and that our souls are going to go on towards eternity. Therefore, we should stay away from things that corrupt them. A Christian adulthood then, should look different to the rest. It shouldn't be defined by destructive alcoholism, drug addiction, promiscuous sex...and not by reckless consumerism either.

Consumerism can partly be blamed on The System again. Because we generally work eight hours a day under The System's terms, we only have evenings and weekends to build a life with. In other words, we are quite short on time. However, the upside of that is we have a little bit of money in our pockets. No time but lots of money means that if we're feeling a little bit dissatisfied with life, we can't cheer ourselves up with things that require time; however, we *can* cheer ourselves up with things that require a bit of money. Therefore, we become accustomed to chasing away our blues by buying things.

I don't just mean buying alcohol, drugs and sex either. We'll buy clothes, shoes, toys, gadgets, new cars and home improvements. Things that, in and of themselves, are not bad. The problem is that we'll do it, not always because we need those things, but simply to cheer ourselves up, to give ourselves a little boost, to keep up with the Joneses, to reward ourselves, to celebrate, to fulfil our childhood vision of what our adulthood would be like, to fix problems, to broadcast our status to the world, to alleviate our boredom and for lots of other psychological reasons. In short, we spend money to manage pain.

In this way, The System actually feeds off our dissatisfaction and *depends* on our willingness to spend as a form of pain management. Because if we're spending, it means businesses are making larger profits. This is why entire marketing departments and specialist advertising agencies will actively cultivate our desire to spend by tapping into the gnawing dissatisfaction in our hearts, and telling us their product will fix it.

We believe them. So we go and buy the bigger car, and television, and get the new clothes, and spend on all manner of things we don't need, looking for the little thrill of excitement that comes with the purchase and which will momentarily mask the emptiness we feel inside. And while there are less terrible things in life than buying a new coat to chase away some blues, when we habitually spend money to numb our pain, we can risk racking up huge debt. That's when this coping mechanism becomes destructive. Furthermore, we're not really getting to the root of the problem and the fact remains that once the thrill of the purchase has gone, we'll still be dissatisfied. Remember, the meaning of life is not to be found in The System.

Escaping Well

Some people will tell you that escapism is always bad, but I don't agree. Only *some* coping mechanisms are bad. Alcoholism, drug abuse, sexual promiscuity and rampant credit card spending are *bad* coping mechanisms. They are *destructive* coping mechanisms that in some cases, will harm your very soul. But nonetheless, we can't get away from the fact that this world is hard, and we simply weren't designed for it, and so even as Christians, we need to develop a coping strategy.

Jesus actually modelled the most effective way of living in a broken world. If you read the gospels you'll notice that he lived according to a very noticeable pattern: he would engage with people for a little while to teach, heal and to do his work, and then he would retreat to a place of solitude to recuperate. Engage, then retreat. Engage, then retreat. Engage, then retreat. It was a tidal rhythm. Luke reports that *"Jesus often withdrew to lonely places and prayed."* The NLT translates the verse similarly saying, *"Jesus often withdrew to the wilderness for prayer."(Luke 5:16) (emphasis added)*

Our culture has cultivated an idolatry of busyness that says you need to stay at the grindstone and any kind of withdrawal from it is a sign of weakness. But constant busyness isn't healthy for us and isn't even very productive.

From a secular perspective, one of the reasons the forty hour week was standardised after the Industrial Revolution was because they discovered worker productivity started plummeting if they were asked to do much more. This is also why companies in The System gladly give their employees at least a few weeks paid time off during the year. And from an equally practical perspective, it's why God, when he created the world, set one day aside and told us to rest in it with his blessing. We actually become more productive when we learn how to incorporate rest into our lives.

Indeed, just as Jesus knew that withdrawing needed to play a key role if he was to be sustained in fulfilling his mission, learning how to escape well might just turn out to be the most productive thing we ever do too. Sometimes in our pride we may like to believe we can stay in the ring with life indefinitely, but even a boxer retreats to the corner between rounds. If we stay engaged for too long without rest, our hearts will soon begin to feel the strain, we'll burn out, and they may even break.

How does one escape well? Well, whatever strengthens our vision of "home" will do the trick. Whatever refreshes our faith or idealism. Whatever brings us back to the threefold meaning of knowing God, loving others, and exploring, learning and ruling over creation.

1 - When Jesus withdrew to lonely places, he wasn't actually alone. He was going to spend time with his Father. Similarly, we can find a lot of refreshment for our spirits when we withdraw from the world periodically to cultivate a personal relationship with God. We do this by finding a quiet place to pray, read the Bible, worship and listen to his voice. If we become intentional in building these retreats into our lives to be with our Father in heaven, that is a great coping mechanism that will actually nourish our souls. In fact, you'll find it to be the best coping mechanism there is.

2 - We can find ourselves refreshed when we spend time with friends and family too. Paul talks about a visit he received from some friends called Stephanas, Fortunatas and Achaicus in the Bible. He says, *"I was glad when [they] arrived...For they refreshed my spirit."* (1 Corinthians 16:17) Spend time with people whom you love and who love you, affirm each other, share your problems, hopes and fears with them, laugh, tell stories, rest in their company, and your spirits will be refreshed.

3 - As for learning, exploring and ruling over creation wisely, well we each have unique interests and there are no limits

to the things we can do to refresh the idealism and faith in our hearts. However, here are some examples:

We can read stories. Read immersive stories that reignite the old truths about romance, good triumphing over evil and windswept adventure. Watch soul nourishing movies too. Watch movies with happy endings that inspire and capture your imagination, and that remind you of better things. Listen to music that doesn't just tell you how ugly the world is; listen to music that tells you of how beautiful the world could be. Travel somewhere delightful and marvel at the stunning scenery which only hints at the glory of the world to come. Dance, sing, learn a new language, play sports, go to art galleries and museums, play with your dog, write poetry, knit, jump on a trampoline, splash through puddles, bake a cake, go to the beach, swim in the ocean, tend a garden, build something with wood, wander through a forest, play the piano, go on a date with your husband or wife, build a snowman, play games...this is a licence to have fun. Even to have childlike fun. It's a licence to come away from the grindstone every now and then, to rest, relax, and to do whatever makes you come alive. God approves of this.

Personally, I love road trips. Scotland is full of beautiful scenery, from the golden sandy beaches on the coasts, to the imposing highland mountains inland, to the ancient green forests, sparkling rivers and lochs, and particularly to my tastes, it is just stuffed full with castles and ancient ruins that date back hundreds, or even thousands of years. There's a romance to it all. I just love getting in the car and driving somewhere to stumble across an old fortress in a remote location, and with no-one else around, letting my imagination be swept away by the stories of what happened there in centuries gone by. I love clambering up inside them and almost feeling like I have time-travelled to another era. I love the silence and the absence of anything from modern life. I can stand there and almost picture medieval knights coming over the horizon, back from a hunting expedition, while the dining hall is readied for a feast. I love the feeling of turning a corner and seeing something new and astonishing on a hilltop in the distance.

Whenever I've been on a road trip and seen some beautiful castle, waterfall, loch, beach, forest or mountainside, I come back refreshed in my spirit and ready to re-engage with the world again. Often, I've been using the silence to talk with God too - I often hear from him the most clearly when I'm outdoors and surrounded by natural beauty - and in a sense it becomes the most productive part of my week or month.

TS Eliot wrote that *"we must not cease from exploration. And the end of all our exploring will be to arrive where we began and to know the place for the first time."*[6] When you withdraw for a while, you come back with a new perspective or understanding, and normally a clearer one too. Wendell Berry wrote well about this too saying, *"When despair for the world grows in me and I wake in the night at the least sound in fear of what my life and my children's lives may be, I go and lie down where the wood drake rests in his beauty on the water, and the great heron feeds. I come into the peace of wild things who do not tax their lives with forethought of grief. I come into the presence of still water. And I feel above me the day-blind stars waiting with their light. For a time I rest in the grace of the world, and am free."*[7]

149

These are just some ideas, but whatever reinvigorates your own sense of idealism, do it. It will give you strength to tackle reality when you come back to re-engage with the world.

Paul summed up what recharges our souls when he said, *"Fix your thoughts on what is true, and honourable, and right, and pure, and lovely, and admirable. Think about things that are excellent and worthy of praise." (Philippians 4:8)* Think about things, focus on things, set your mind on things, meditate upon things that remind you of all the good you innately believed before the world started trying to beat it out of you.

And don't feel embarrassed about whatever gives you joy either. Recently there was a craze for adult colouring books. I don't know how widespread this craze was but it seemed adults everywhere just suddenly rediscovered a long forgotten pleasure in it. I heard many, even from church platforms, ridiculing this practice as a horrendous and unproductive waste of time, but I'm prone to disagree with them. A brief period of non-productivity can, in the end, be very productive indeed. And I'm prone to disagree with those who belittle things like that as being too childish. Children often know how to have the best fun of all!

Furthermore, this is why I'm prone to disagree with anyone who views all escapism as a pitiful crutch for the cowardly and weak. The truth is that someone attempts to kill themselves by jumping off Brooklyn Bridge in New York every fifteen days because of broken hearts. These are people for whom reality became too much to handle, their hope died, their spirits were crushed, and they couldn't find the strength to go on. Imagine how many more souls would be claimed the same way, if not for the existence of dreams and the opportunity to escape into them from time-to-time? Whatever gives you strength to come back and keep going, don't feel ashamed of it.

So it turns out there's bad escapism and there's good escapism. The Russian playwright, Anton Chekhov once wrote plaintively, *"Why are we worn out? Why do we, who start out so passionate, brave, noble, believing, become totally bankrupt by the age of thirty of thirty-five? Why is that one is extinguished by consumption, another puts a bullet in his head, a third seeks oblivion in vodka or cards, a fourth, in order to stifle fear and anguish, cynically tramples underfoot the portrait of his pure, beautiful youth? Why is it, that once fallen, we do not try to rise, and, having lost one thing, we do not seek another? Why?"*[8]

Chekhov is talking about people who haven't learned to retreat well here, and who have turned to vodka and gambling to cope with life, or people who have even put a bullet through their heads because they couldn't take it anymore. And while Chekhov is confused by this - that we should all start off so full of hope in life and yet get so worn out - hopefully we're not so confused. Hopefully we're not going to turn to such destructive coping mechanisms either. And hopefully through positive ones that reinforce our vision of home, we're all now ready to stay strong well into adulthood. In short, hopefully we're learning how to withdraw well.

Remember To Re-Engage

Just remember to re-engage. That's all. Remember that as many times as Jesus withdrew to the wilderness, he always came back again. His withdrawals were never to keep him from doing his work, they were only to strengthen him to do his work better.

I say this because when we escape, we will probably like the place we escape to more than we like real life. If we escape to a quiet, beautiful place in the countryside to be with God; if we escape to cosy family environments; if we escape into a book that has us placed on some Caribbean island or if we escape into a movie that has us roaming galaxies and discovering new worlds, we may not be very keen to come back to reality to deal with taxes, dishwashing, boredom, hostile enemies and news reports of terrorism. But if we don't come back into the real world, we'll be of no use whatsoever. And furthermore, our escapism may start to damage our real lives.

If you're a mum who spends hours on Facebook while neglecting your children; if you're a wife who gets so lost in romance fiction that you no longer spend enough time investing in a real relationship with your husband; if you're a gamer who loves digital worlds so much that you're neglecting your school work; then it's time to bring some balance back and re-engage with the world.

I know about this from first-hand experience. When I was growing up, as I described earlier, I used to play video games a lot with Brendan and loved getting lost in digital worlds. In fact, as I entered into my twenties and saw more of reality, I discovered that I sometimes enjoyed being in a digital world more than the real one!

I was particularly partial to a football management simulator called, well...Football Manager...and would spend hours and hours on this game. I'd be scouting players, trading players, tweaking training regimes, fixing contracts, expanding stadiums and trying to win as many titles as possible long into the night - sometimes until 2am or 3am. I was so enamoured with this fantasy world where I'd become a famous soccer coach that I found it difficult to switch off and come away from it. In fact, I discovered that I was spending so much time in that fake world that I was no longer doing anything of much use in the real one! Furthermore, playing the game had kept me *from* doing important things in the real one. I was tired and was sleeping through my alarm, and I was daydreaming about tactics and player purchases when I was meant to be doing university coursework. When it started negatively impacting my life like that, I decided that was no longer a healthy kind of escape for me. It had become a destructive one. I had to force myself back to more of reality and I actually stopped playing video games from that moment on.

So we have to be careful with this. If you have a type of escape that keeps you from coming back to reality refreshed and re-energised, it may be time to reassess what you're doing. Technology experts tell us that we're on the cusp of a Virtual Reality boom and in the years ahead we're all going to be wearing headsets that will allow us to enter into fully immersive digital worlds. We'll feel like we're really there. Of course, while VR isn't inherently bad, if we become so immersed in virtual worlds that we prefer it to the real one, we'll soon find people living out their entire lives there. It will become a brand new form of pain management for reclusive individuals who can't face the responsibility of operating outside their four walls. We have to walk carefully with such things. Whatever we do, however we retreat, we must remember to come back and re-engage.

How often should we withdraw then? Well, since God gave us one day in every seven to rest, that's a pretty good marker. Perhaps by that measure, some of us will need to rest more than we realise, and some of us will need to work more than we realise! That's for each of us to decide.

Particularly be careful about anything that distracts you from doing the work God has set in front of you. Satan will use these for his own purposes. Sometimes when I'm writing or creating a series, I'll go onto YouTube to find research material, and the temptation is to start watching some fluff instead. Sometimes I'll go onto the Fuel Facebook page to find something important and end up scrolling through memes and pictures of cats. This is why we need to be intentional and controlled with our escapism. Engage, retreat. Engage, retreat. Engage, retreat. We need balance.

Apologies for another Braveheart reference but you may remember a scene where William Wallace is dreaming of being with his dead wife, Murron. They're in a beautiful forest together, it's peaceful and calm and he is cherishing being in her company. Somewhere in his subconscious, he knows he must be dreaming and so he tells her, "I'm dreaming." Murron tells him that he is, and explains he can't stay there forever: "You must wake." William replies, "I don't want to wake. I want to stay here with you." It's peaceful with Murron in the dream world. It's cosy. It's warm. It's refreshing. And yet he must awake. He must wake up and go back to reality. He must re-engage. He must go back to the hard reality where his true love is actually dead, and where he is a wanted man; where he is tired and hungry and cold; and where his mission is to keep fighting for freedom against terrible odds.

I can imagine when Jesus was in retreat spending time with his Father, how he might have found it similarly difficult to go back to reality too. He must have so enjoyed those moments away from the crowds. And I guess he sometimes wouldn't have relished the idea of going back to them - a stiff-necked people who slandered him, rejected him and tried to throw him off crags when he told them the truth. Indeed, people who before long were due to betray him and crucify him. And yet Jesus did always re-engage, because he knew he had work to do.

Let me use one last analogy to explain why both engaging and retreating is so important: Imagine you're a soldier in a fierce and vicious war. Imagine that you're in a dystopian wasteland of dirt, barbed wire, mines, gunfire, explosions and death. You've witnessed a lot of tragedy during this war. You've lost close friends on the battlefield and you've experienced much in the way of sleep deprivation, thirst and hunger. Every day you wake up knowing that this might be your last day on earth, and to top it off you've been away from home for a long time. You're missing your family and your friends, and it's been a long, hard battle.

You can only handle those stressful living conditions for so long before your performance starts to suffer, so occasionally your commanding officer takes you away from the frontline and lets you stay at the base to recuperate. You love those days because it's the only time you get any restful sleep. And sleeping is mostly what you do.

On one of these sleeps, you drift off into deep in a wonderful dream. You're dreaming about being back home with your family, and it's a peaceful and contented scene. You have hot food on the table and a warm bed to sleep in at nights. The air is fresh and clean and there are hot showers and dry clothes. The scenery is beautiful around your home and you can wander outside under the sunshine and the clear blue skies without any fear. You love being in that dream - it feels so real - and you just never want to leave.

All of a sudden, your commanding officer rushes into your room and tells you the enemy are close and you need to get back to the frontline. He orders you to grab your gun and get back to your position immediately.

Your heart sinks. You don't really want to go back to the frontline at all. You wish you could close your eyes again, shut out reality, and live in your dream instead. You were happy in your dream. It felt like you belonged there. You hate all this war and turmoil and you just want to be released from it. You crave home like nothing else.

And yet, that's not what this is all about. You have work to do here. There's a war to win. You're in the battle to change reality for millions of oppressed people and you can't stop fighting until the mission is complete. You put on your boots, grab your gun, and head back to the frontline, knowing you'll do your duty until the day the war ends, or the day your commanding officer calls you to go home for good.

For a Christian, we should be like that soldier dreaming of home. We understand we're in a fallen world with pain, we see it everywhere we look, we know we don't belong here and we ache to go home and live in peace, but in the meantime, we know we're here with work to do. And we must get on with doing it. We must go about changing reality for all the lost souls on this earth, defeating the powers of darkness. God will tell us when we're done and we won't be done a moment before. We can only use the vision of home to spur us on.

Paul wrote about this dichotomy of Christian life to the Philippians saying, *"I will continue to be bold for Christ, as I have been in the past. And I trust that my life will bring honour to Christ, whether I live or die. For to me, living means living for Christ, and dying is even better. But if I live, I can do more fruitful works for Christ. So I really don't know which is better. I'm torn between two desires: I long to go and be with Christ, which would be far better for me. But for your sakes, it is better that I continue to live." (Philippians 1:20-24)*

Paul is saying that while he lives, he will glorify Jesus Christ and fight to change reality, but actually, there's a part of him that wants to be done with the struggle and wants to go home already. He says that he would actually love to leave this world behind and be with his Saviour. Our attitude should mirror Paul's.

And of course, as we know, Paul indeed worked tirelessly travelling around Asia Minor and Europe, teaching, debating, reasoning, discipling, pastoring, writing and doing whatever else was necessary to establish the gospel. I dare say he copied Jesus' tidal rhythm of engaging and retreating as he went. That tidal rhythm saw Paul through to the end of his days and it'll do the same for us.

Through A Child's Eyes

One more quick thing about adulthood before we finish this chapter and move on. It's likely that by the end of your thirties you will have children of your own, and this will probably have a reinvigorating effect on you.

You see, having children will allow you to see the world afresh again through their unaffected eyes. You'll watch their eyes light up when they see a bumblebee for the first time and it'll remind you of the small wonders of life that you've become numb to through familiarity. They'll splash in puddles and laugh, so you'll splash in puddles too and remember what a simple pleasure it is. They'll bounce on trampolines, so you'll bounce on them too, and ask yourself why you ever stopped doing this yourself. They'll want to go to the park and waste time by looking at flowers and feeding the ducks, so you'll go with them, and enjoy the simple pleasures of life once again. Their childlike sense of fun and mischief will resurrect some of the best parts of your personality that life has eroded. In a sense, they will bring part of your youth back to life.

Sir Alex Ferguson, who is now considered one of the greatest sports team managers of all time and who now regularly shares his secrets of management at Harvard University, famously managed to sustained success at the top for over thirty years. He was often asked about what kept him so full of energy to compete season-after-season. His drive was so legendary that he was still doing it, and still winning trophies, into his seventies. His response to that question was always telling. He always said it was the young players he worked with that kept him young inside. He saw their enthusiasm and their energy and it rubbed off on him. He was worried about the day when he retired because he wouldn't be around young people anymore, and he thought it might speed up his own ageing process.

And so it seems that children are good for adults, in ways we often don't realise. We think we're bringing them into the world to do everything for them and that it's something of a one-way street, but there's a way in which they're doing much for us too. They're reminding us of the hopeful, joyful creatures we were made to be, and the kind of hopeful, joyful creatures we will one day be again.

What's more, they tend to come along at just the right time. In the same way that first love arrives just as we are entering into the bereavement of teenage angst and it all looks too bleak for us to handle, children come around the time the first wave of life is over, and we've perhaps started to realise that living for ourselves really isn't worth it. We're starting to discover perhaps, that we're only really happy when we're living to glorify God, loving others and engaged in some meaningful work. Kids come along to help us out with the second of those endeavours, and when they do, a second wave of life begins. A second wave marked by responsibility and love.[9]

Chapter Seven

Growing Old

"It's paradoxical that the idea of living a long life appeals to everyone, but the idea of getting old doesn't appeal to anyone." - Andy Rooney

"A man doesn't grow old because he has lived a certain number of years. A man grows old when he deserts his ideal. The years may wrinkle his skin, but deserting his ideal wrinkles his soul." - Brennan Manning

---

There's a law of Physics at work in the universe called the Second Law of Thermodynamics. Basically, it can be summed up as the Law of Decay and it states that the whole universe naturally moves from a state of order to chaos.

Now this law touches absolutely everything. It's the reason why food goes mouldy; it's why fences break, glass shatters and roofs develop holes; it's why hot drinks get cold; it's why clothes become threadbare; it's why we need to go to hospital to get treatment for illnesses, and in the end, it's even why we grow old and die. The Second Law of Thermodynamics teaches us that everything in the universe slowly breaks down over time. Everything moves towards chaos. Everything ultimately decays, disintegrates, decomposes and dies.

The best way to picture the Second Law of Thermodynamics in action is to imagine building a sandcastle on the beach. As you build the castle, you are effectively bringing a kind of form to millions of disordered grains of sand. You are bringing order into the chaos. And when you're finished, they will temporarily sit in a structured way that resembles a castle of your design. However, if you then leave that castle to the elements, it will almost immediately begin to disintegrate again. The wind will blow away the grains, the whole structure will erode, and eventually it will turn back into a chaotic, disordered mound of sand. This is the Second Law of Thermodynamics in action - *everything* moves from order to chaos.

We humans are always fighting against this law, of course. We're always trying to come up with ways to preserve food for longer; we have a DIY industry to help keep our properties from falling into ruins; we invented the thermos to stop hot drinks from getting cold; we stitch and sew so that we don't walk around in threadbare rags, and we devise medicines to stop our bodies from breaking down and dying before necessary. In the most extreme cases, people have even had their dead bodies cryogenically frozen in the hope that The Second Law of Thermodynamics will one day be overcome forever and they can be brought back to life.

However we go about it, it takes a lot of time and energy to fight against this Law of Decay, and ultimately it's a war that, physically at least, we never win. The food *will* eventually go mouldy in the end despite our best efforts; our buildings may last for centuries but they *will* eventually need renovation or collapse in ruins; hot drinks *will* eventually get cold even in a thermos; clothes *will* eventually need to be replaced altogether; and the medicines for our illnesses will only postpone the inevitable. The truth is, we will all grow old, and we will all die.

This appeals to absolutely no-one. No-one wants to get older and experience decay in their own bodies. Sure, we want to live forever...but in imperishable frames. No-one relishes the idea that they're going to become less mobile, less agile, less beautiful and strong. And when we catch sight of our own mortality for the first time, it can cause our hearts to sink in despair. The first time we spot a grey hair, or see some wrinkles that weren't there before, or notice we're taking longer to recover from heavy workouts, or find we need glasses to help our weakening eyes read the news, we are reminded in some small yet devastating way that life isn't going to last forever.

Science Confirms The Biblical Narrative

Now the fact the Second Law of Thermodynamics exists at all should point us towards God, because you'll notice that it fits the Biblical narrative perfectly. Genesis 1:1 says, *"In the beginning God created the heavens and the earth. The earth was formless and empty...."* The rest of the chapter then explains how God starts bringing form into the formless earth - order, structure, design...like a human building a sandcastle on the beach but to the nth degree of difficulty - until eventually he looks and sees that every part of what he has made is perfect. Next God places Man and Woman into the perfectly ordered paradise, and as we know, it isn't long before Satan tempts them into The Fall. From that moment, we know that Eden is lost, and degradation begins undoing the flawless design God had established. The universe starts moving from order to chaos. The Second Law of Thermodynamics is at work. Therefore, we immediately start reading about pain, suffering, shame, lies, murder, betrayal, natural disasters and disease, and we are told in no uncertain terms that the world has begun slowly unravelling.

The Bible goes on to explain how mankind tries to fight against the decay by building embryonic versions of The System to prop up society. We read about kings who try to rule in the absence of God but somehow, despite their best efforts, their own flaws and the deterioration of the world at large sees it all come crashing down again. And this keeps happening over and over. Mankind just can't seem to overcome the chaos. CS Lewis wrote, *"This is the key to history. Terrific energy is expended-civilisations are built up-excellent institutions devised; but each time something goes wrong. Some fatal flaw always brings the selfish and cruel people to the top and it all slides back into misery and ruin. In fact, the machine conks. It seems to start up all right and runs a few yards, and then it breaks down. They are trying to run it on the wrong juice. That is what Satan has done to us humans."*[1]

By the time we reach the end of the Bible, we are given a prophetic insight into how it will all end. Revelation gives us a vision of an apocalyptic planet that has come to complete ruins - physically, morally and socially. Formlessness is returning and the earth is in its death throes. Cataclysmic natural disasters are destroying the life on land and sea, men and women have become more wicked than we can yet imagine, diseases and pestilences are running rampant across the face of the earth, and the very fabric of creation appears to be breaking up.

In other words, the Bible teaches what the Second Law of Thermodynamics confirms - things will decay. Secular scientists today predict that the universe has a remaining lifespan of five billion years. They postulate that all the usable energy within it is gradually becoming redundant and when that happens, all creation will effectively die. The stars will grow dark and burn out, and as our own sun wanes, plants here will cease to grow, animals will perish, and life on earth will fail to flourish. All will become formless and empty once more, just as it had been in the first verse of Genesis.

Speaking from a Christian perspective, I don't believe it will take anywhere near five billion years for the apocalyptic events of Revelation to take hold. But either way, if our hearts weren't sunk by the first glimpse of our own mortality, there is something perhaps even more terminal and horrifying about the idea the entire universe will end. It turns out that even if we did manage to bring the cryogenically frozen back to life, they still wouldn't live forever. Death would still have the final say. Death it seems, is always destined to have the final say.

There's much to say about this, but we should begin by asking a simple question: If the whole universe naturally tends towards chaos and death, then who brought the initial order and life? What I mean is, if it takes an intelligent mind to bring order to grains of sand on the beach in the form of a simple sandcastle, then surely it follows that it takes intelligence to bring order to an entire universe that is bent on going in the opposite direction?

This is why the Psalmist wrote, *"the heavens proclaim the glory of God. The skies display his craftsmanship. Day after day they continue to speak; night after night they make him known. They speak without a sound or word; their voice is never heard. Yet their message has gone throughout the earth, and their words to all the world." (Psalm 19:1-4)* This is why Paul wrote, *"For ever since the world was created, people have seen the earth and the sky. Through everything God made, they can clearly see his invisible qualities - his eternal power and divine nature. So they have no excuse for not knowing God." (Romans 1:20)* The ordered, life-filled design of the universe screams to us about the existence of a designer. And once this simple fact is understood, it leaves no room for atheism at all.

For the theory of evolution to be true, the laws of Physics would need to be completely turned upside down. You see, the theory of evolution is predicated upon the idea that the universe is naturally moving from *chaos* to *order*. It proposes that things less complex than ourselves adapted, evolved, acquired new biological information, and became *more* sophisticated and structured throughout a course of billions of years. It says this happened without any intelligent intervention at all. In other words, from an amoeba in a primordial pond in the distant mists of time, came forth a random progression of evermore sophisticated, yet entirely accidental creatures, until we arrived at things we'd recognise today: monkeys, dogs, penguins, pandas, hedgehogs and even human beings.

Now, if you know that sandcastles don't build themselves on the beach accidentally but instead come from an intelligent mind; if you know working jet planes don't assemble themselves accidentally from junkyards but instead come from intelligent minds; if you know that books, microchips and paintings don't evolve accidentally but instead come from intelligent minds, then you'll know that complex, well designed, intelligent creatures like ourselves didn't evolve accidentally either, but instead must have come from an intelligent mind.

And indeed, it's important to state that science has *never* observed the movement from chaos to order that evolution describes. No creature has *ever* been observed to randomly acquire new biological information that added to its complexity, sophistication, or ability to function in the world in a more efficient way. In fact, quite the opposite.

Biological studies have always confirmed the Second Law of Thermodynamics by explaining how all life is currently subject to random genetic mutations that *subtract* information from our structured DNA code. Therefore, we are, as a human race, becoming more prone to disease and dysfunction as the generations go by. Very simply, all good science supports the idea of *devolution* rather than evolution. Therefore, although it was an intriguing concept some two hundred years ago when Charles Darwin first published *The Origin of Species*, science has moved on, the theory of evolution has become outdated, and those who still subscribe to it, have got their thinking back-to-front. *Everything* decays and ultimately dies.

If we could visualise it on a graph, the two worldviews would look a bit like this:

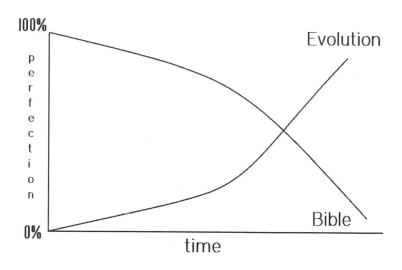

Death Brings Futility

Now since the Second Law of Thermodynamics dictates that decay and death must come to us and the entire universe, we are now forced to admit that all life is actually futile. Devastatingly futile. That's the worst thing about death. Not only is it guaranteed to end our lives but it somehow reaches into life too, and renders our efforts within it completely meaningless.

So what if we strive courageously and achieve great things? So what if we feel deeply, and dare to hope and dream? So what if we bravely conquer fears and have our characters refined by failures? So what if we love passionately? So what if we laugh or cry? So what if we aspire to the highest ideals and create beautiful works of poetry, art and music? So what if we uncover the secrets of the universe and expand our hearts and minds? So what if we right wrongs and struggle against the troubles of life to achieve some good? So what if we overcome adversity to triumph against all odds? So what if we live a long life or a short one? It doesn't matter in the end. Nothing really matters in the end. Because everything dies in the end anyway.

Jackson Burnett wrote, *"A thousand years from now nobody is going to know that you or I ever lived. The cynic is right...He says, "You live, you die and nothing you do will ever make a difference."*[2] William Shakespeare famously described life as *"all sound and fury and signifying nothing."*[3] Death brings a despairing futility to everything it touches, and it means that the human experience, both our best and worst moments, really does ultimately signify *nothing*. After all, if in five billion years the universe is lying empty and cold, it will be like none of this ever happened.

Realising this, even in some small way, can leave us feeling hugely discouraged and even depressed. Remember, we started off as children who felt like we'd arrived here to inherit the earth, and that it would be ours forever. We had such hope in our hearts. It seemed somehow that all of human history had just been a precursor to our appearance and now we were here, we would live forever.

And now it turns out it's all just going to fade away?!

Well, what's it all for? What is there to hope for? Where's our meaning for existence? We need to be able to answer that question because if we can't we're doomed. Human beings need something to hope for. Indeed, if there's one thing that a human being, perhaps indeed any living thing, can't survive without, it's hope. We *need* hope. We need to believe that no matter how difficult things may be in the present, that they can be better in the future. Hope is the fuel that keeps our hearts pumping - it's our life support system. It's what keeps our idealism alive. It's what fuels our faith. Hope is what allows us to witness all the pain of life, and acknowledge its reality, but still believe that some good can come of it all. It's what keeps us going in all circumstances.

In fact, it's as stark as this: place a person in the bleakest and most tragic situation you can imagine, and as long as they have hope in their hearts, I can guarantee they'll get through it somehow. Their vision of something better ahead will sustain them even in the darkest hours. However, the moment they lose that hope and the future begins to look terminally bleak, they'll go into a swift decline and almost certainly won't make it through. We simply have no heart for a fight we have no hope of winning.

Solomon hints at this when he says, *"The human spirit can endure a sick body, but who can bear a crushed spirit?" (Proverbs 18:14)* and *"A cheerful heart is good medicine, but a broken spirit saps a person's strength." (Proverbs 17:22)* We can only get through life if we have *hope*. Realising this, the current suicide statics should make a lot of sense:4

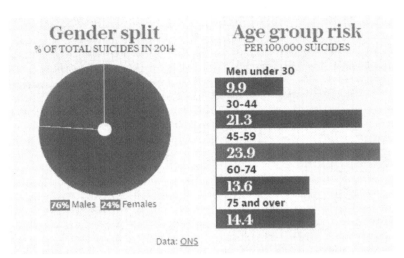

Gender split
% OF TOTAL SUICIDES IN 2014

76% Males 24% Females

Age group risk
PER 100,000 SUICIDES

Men under 30
9.9
30-44
21.3
45-59
23.9
60-74
13.6
75 and over
14.4

Data: ONS

What you are looking at here, are statistics of people who lost hope. And notice a spike as they hit middle-age. Why do people appear to lose hope in their late 40s and 50s in particular? Why do they become so despairing?

The reason is because people in this age bracket have been in the middle of the fight for some time now and it's not always been easy; life's blows have been landing for decades; they've toiled to overcome the Second Law of Thermodynamics throughout; they've kept beautifying their surroundings and decorating their homes and tidying their gardens and they've battled to preserve order from encroaching chaos; they've experienced many disappointments and failures, but they've struggled hard to get up and keep going in the hope they can achieve things; maybe they've landed some blows of their own and had some successes and changed some realities along the way; maybe they've felt that despite all the pain, they've been winning at life in some small way, or as though there was always a distant star up ahead for them to strive for...but then they've suddenly caught a glimpse of their own mortality and of death itself, and the fight has left their hearts. The 'sound and fury' of life they could deal with, but it's the realisation that the sound and fury signifies nothing that kills them. They realise that it doesn't matter if they win some battles because they're going to lose the war.

They realise that actually, nothing matters. Death will win and render all their goals, ambitions, achievements and endeavours meaningless. It's inevitable. No-one can beat death or undo the futility death brings to life. So why are they even fighting at all? Why keep slogging? Why go on? As Solomon rightly stated when he wrote Ecclesiastes, if there is no God but only an oblivion beyond, then *"Everything is meaningless... completely meaningless!" (Ecclesiastes 1:2)*

Most adults, of course, don't resort to the extreme of suicide, but they will show signs of bereavement for their youth. Remember, the bereavement process is Denial, Anger, Bargaining, Depression, Acceptance. In adolescents we called it 'teenage angst' and in midlifers we know it as a 'midlife crisis'. A midlifer in crisis may live in denial of the ageing process and of the death it leads to, and try to scramble back to their youth. They may get botox and cosmetic surgery in a bid to mask the effects of time. They may get nostalgic and try to recapture their lost youth through music, sports cars, motorbikes, tattoos, growing their hair long, taking up extreme sports, and suchlike. The depression aspect of bereavement may also reveal itself in a heavy spirit, a diminishing zest for life, increased cynicism, and all the coping mechanisms we mentioned in the previous chapter: Drinking, smoking, gambling, drug addiction, reckless consumerism and suchlike.

Perhaps the most common coping mechanism for adults growing older however, is just to bury their heads in the sand. It's to busy themselves and to stay preoccupied with short-term life.

It's often been said that the scariest part of the day for many adults is that moment at night between the lights going out and falling asleep, because in the still quietness of their solitude, they have nothing to distract their minds from the far-sighted issues of life. Where will we go when we die? Are we sure of what comes next? Many refuse to even acknowledge these questions, and perhaps still scarier for them is the gentle but persistent voice of God whispering to their souls in those moments, telling them truths about their eternal destinies that they don't want to hear. Some use white noise, the radio, or ambient sounds to block out the silence and to focus their minds on something...anything...other than what life really means. Instead, they deliberately live short-sightedly, allowing themselves to become consumed by trivialities - what to have for dinner at night, what outfit they're going to wear on Saturday, and how they're going to get that promotion and secure that raise. To use a Biblical metaphor, they spend their days entirely focused on expanding their barns and filling them with grain.

Often when I wander round the castle ruins in Scotland, I think about this. I think of all the fighting and feuding the kings and noblemen went through to establish their names on the earth. I think of the betrayals and killings that went on to make sure their kingdom became pre-eminent, and the way they built these massive fortresses as a show of their wealth and prestige, and then I consider as I see the now shattered, desolate ruins, how short-sighted they all were to live that way. After all, it has all come to nothing, and they themselves all now lie dead in the ground, and the world has moved on without them.

What was it really all for? I wonder, if they could see that all their scheming, feuding and building has come to nought, and that their kingdoms have disappeared, and that their mighty fortresses are now dilapidated tourist attractions, would they have been happy with the way they lived their lives? To be honest, I think they'd feel a little embarrassed that they got so caught up in short-sighted, worldly, trivial affairs. Because while they were striving for all that this world could offer and trampling on each other to make it happen, it's of no use to them now. It's all passed away, just the same as they have.

We should learn from our ancestor's mistakes, but we rarely do. Most people today - certainly unbelievers - still bury their heads in the sand and continue to live as though they have come to inherit the earth, and as though it'll be theirs forever. They too refuse to look too far into the future and instead strive, and war, and feud, and worry about material things, and build their empires, and accumulate their wealth in a futile bid to establish their names on the earth. But as they build bigger barns and stuff them with grain, one day God will say to them, *"You fool! You will die this very night. Then who will get everything you worked for? Yes, a person is a fool to store up earthly wealth but not have a rich relationship with God." (Luke 12:20-21)*

The truth is that our lives are just as fleeting as those who have gone before us. Indeed, our lives are like a wisp of smoke in the wind - here at this moment, but then potentially gone before the next sunrise. James describes it like a morning mist. So how foolish to live as though this world is all that matters, and as though we're going to live *here* forever. The only thing that matters is the only thing that's ever mattered, and that's developing a relationship with our Lord, who we are depending upon for everlasting life, and who has promised to lead us to our real eternal home.

Jesus Brings Meaning

So you see what this means now? If death renders all life futile, the only life that can have any meaning is the eternal one. Therefore, if we are to have any solid hope for the future, the inescapable fact is that we need to live forever. We just need to. There's nothing else for it. Death *needs* to be conquered somehow.

Of course, we can't do that. But thankfully we don't need to, because Jesus has already done it on our behalf. Jesus came to earth to die on a cross and on the third day, he was resurrected in an incorruptible body. Through him who conquered the grave, we too can now live forever.

Jesus said, *"I am the resurrection and the life. Anyone who lives in me will live, even after dying. Everyone who lives in me and believes in me will never ever die." (John 11:25)* The most famous verse in the Bible says, *"For God so loved the world that he gave his one and only begotten Son, so that everyone who believes in him will not perish but have eternal life." (John 3:16)* Jesus again said, *"Don't let your hearts be troubled...I am going to prepare a place for you. When everything is ready, I will come and get you, so that you will always be with me where I am." (John 14:1-3)*

Jesus brings hope back into our lives by giving us eternal life. And because life is now eternal, as it was always meant to be, our days on *this* earth have now been refilled with meaning. Forgive me if I labour this point but it's vital we get this: If we were to ultimately die, *nothing* we would do would have any significance; but if we're to live forever then the opposite is true: *everything* we do suddenly has *eternal* significance.

In the light of eternity, if we strive courageously and achieve great things; if we dare to hope and dream; if we bravely conquer fears and have our character's refined from failures; if we love passionately; if we laugh or cry; if we aspire to the highest ideals and create beautiful works of poetry, art and music; if we uncover the secrets of the universe and expand our hearts and mind; if we right wrongs and struggle against the troubles of life to do some good; if we overcome adversity to triumph against all odds...it all means something and it means something *forever! Everything* we do is now packed with meaning through Jesus Christ, and indeed, all of our thoughts, words and deeds suddenly have *eternal* significance. I guess if I can state it in one final way, it's this: If life ends, nothing within it matters, but if life doesn't end, everything within it matters, and matters eternally. Even our struggles. Indeed, maybe *especially* our struggles.

The Wilderness Before The Promised Land

I often get asked why God is allowing the world to keep spinning when it's clearly unravelling. Why doesn't Jesus come back today? Why doesn't he intervene and stop it all now? Why wait? Well, you'll notice in the Bible that before the Lord leads anyone to a promised land, they must walk through a wilderness first.

Take Abraham, for example. Abraham was told that he was going to be 'the father of many nations' and that he would be 'extremely fruitful.' One clear, starry night, "...*the Lord took [Abraham] outside and said to him, 'Look up into the sky and count the stars if you can. That's how many descendants you will have!" (Genesis 15:5)* That was a kind of 'promised land' for Abraham.

Of course, we next read that Abraham and his wife Sarah spent many years struggling to conceive a child, and for a long time it seemed as though God's promise would never come true. That was their wilderness. It was a time of waiting on the Lord in difficult circumstances, surviving on their faith alone that God would stay true to his word, but grappling with fear, doubt and despair along the way.

The Bible tells us that one day their faith, in fact, faltered, and they tried to force the issue by having a child through Sarah's handmaid Hagar. That didn't work out to well. In fact, it only created more problems, and they remained in the wilderness. They were in the wilderness for so long that Abraham reached one-hundred-years of age and Sarah, ninety! Surely their promised land was beyond reach now?

But no. Again the Lord came back to Abraham and said, *'Your descendants will become many nations, and kings will be among them!' (Genesis 17:5-6)* God doesn't just reaffirm the promise but he *adds* to it. *Kings* will be among the descendants!

Abraham's response though, was one of a man who was losing hope. He was becoming cynical in his old age. The Bible says, *"Abraham laughed to himself in disbelief. 'How could I become a father at the age of 100?' he thought. 'And how can Sarah have a baby when she is ninety years old?'" (Genesis 17:17)* It seemed impossible. And yet God stayed true to his word and the promised land finally arrived when Sarah gave birth to Isaac. We know the rest: Isaac was the father of Jacob, and Jacob's sons became the fathers of the twelve tribes of Israel, and Abraham's descendants became as numerous as the stars in the sky. And Jesus, the king of Kings, were among them.

Let's take one of Jacob's sons, Joseph, as another example of a wilderness before a promised land. When Joseph was perhaps around seventeen-years-old, he was given a prophetic dream about his future that suggested that he was going to become a person of great power and influence. That was his 'promised land'.

However, before Joseph reached that promised land, he was beaten up by his jealous brothers, thrown into a pit, sold into slavery, falsely accused of sexually molesting his master's wife, and then thrown into prison. That was his wilderness.

Like Abraham, Joseph had to wait a long time in the wilderness. He spent years in that prison and at times his teenage dreams must have seemed to mock him. And yet, maybe around thirteen years after receiving those dreams, he was finally released and made to be Pharaoh's right-hand man in Egypt - he became at that time one of the most powerful men in the ancient world. He reached his promised land.

Another example. After Joseph's death, his descendants became enslaved in Egypt, and so God raised up Moses to free them. Moses, who himself had spent forty years in the wilderness as a shepherd prior this defining moment of his life, was told by God, *"I have come down to rescue them from the power of the Egyptians and lead them out of Egypt into their own fertile and spacious land. It is a land flowing with milk and honey..."* *(Exodus 3:8)* So God used Moses to lead the Hebrew people out of Egypt towards the promised land...but they didn't get there right away. Between Egypt and Canaan was the Sinai desert, and God kept them in that desert for a long time. In fact, *"The Lord...made them wander in the wilderness for forty years..."* *(Numbers 32:13)* before he permitted them to enter their new home.

Another example. Not long after Israel had become established in their homeland, David was anointed to be the future king of Israel. David was just a boy at this time, indeed the youngest in his family. The Lord told the prophet Samuel to go and tell him that he would one day rule over the entire nation. That was his 'promised land'. And yet, he didn't become king right away. David had to literally run to the wilderness to escape the jealous Saul, where he lived in caves and hid with fear. The depths of despair David found himself in are evident when you read some of the Psalms which he wrote during those dark times, and that wilderness actually lasted for many years. However, eventually he did become king of Israel. He reached his promised land.

John the Baptist famously lived in the wilderness prior to beginning his ministry, and even Jesus himself went through this process. He came to teach, die and to rise again, and he was aware of this destiny from early childhood. But before he stepped into his ministry at around thirty-years-old, *"Jesus was led by the Spirit into the wilderness to be tempted there by the devil."* *(Matthew 4:1)* Even Jesus had to go through the wilderness experience to prove himself ready for the responsibility of his mission. After all, it was a mission that would require an unprecedented level of courage and obedience.

So you see, before any 'promised land' - before God gives anyone some kind of responsibility, or leads them into their destiny - he will almost certainly lead them to the wilderness first. The reason is that the wilderness refines our characters and moulds us into the kind of people we need to be to support the destiny he has for us. And this is why even our struggles are good for us in the light of eternity. Paul wrote that because *"we confidently and joyfully look forward to sharing God's glory...We can rejoice too when we run into problems and trials, for we know that they help us develop endurance. And endurance develops strength of character, and character strengthens our confident hope of salvation. And this hope will not lead to disappointment. For we know how dearly God loves us, because he has given us the Holy Spirit to fill our hearts with love."* *(Romans 5:1-5)*

In the same way that tumultuous water turns a jagged rock into a smooth pebble; in the same way that fire purifies gold; in the same way that resistance makes our muscles strong; going through turmoil and struggle in life refines our characters and produces within us a magnificent resilience. We are made beautiful and strong by our trials; we are being prepared to 'share in God's glory'. Therefore, the wilderness before a promised land theory doesn't just apply to the destiny God has for us on *this* earth, it applies to the destiny we're all going to share in when we go home to be with Jesus on the new earth. In other words, this *whole* life, with all its toils and snares, can simply be seen as a wilderness before heaven.

The Christian Juxtaposition

You might be able to see a stark juxtaposition in the Christian life now. Even though we are physically subject to the Second Law of Thermodynamics like everyone else and our bodies are still subject to decay and death, we believe there is an inner part of us that is going to live forever through Christ. We would call that part of us 'the soul' perhaps. In Genesis we read, *"And the Lord God formed man of the dust of the ground, and breathed into his nostrils the breath of life; and man became a living soul."* *(Genesis 2:7)(KJV)* Man was effectively just a bag of bones until this moment. It was the soul that was the essence of his life. And though the body was made from dust and will return to dust, the soul came from God and will return to God.

So remember how I said in the previous chapter that even though our bodies age, there's an inner part of us that always seems to stay the same? That's because that part of us is actually ageless! It's our eternal soul. And through our life experiences, it's that part of us which is being made beautiful and strong in Jesus. Indeed, our souls are being fitted for heaven.

Paul wrote to the Corinthians saying, *"Therefore we do not lose heart. Though outwardly we are wasting away, yet inwardly we are being renewed each day. For our light and momentary troubles are achieving for us an eternal glory that far outweighs them all. So we fix our eyes not on what is seen, but on what is unseen, since what is seen is temporary, but what is unseen is eternal."* (2 Corinthians 4:16-18) If we could put that down on a chart, it would look something like this:

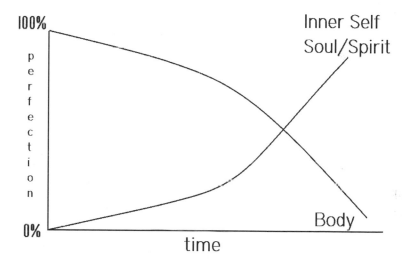

One part of us is devolving while the other is evolving. One part of us is dying while the other part is just coming to life. Therefore it's no wonder that as we move through time, one part of that experience feels alien to us and another part feels perfectly natural - namely that none of us wants to grow old but we all want to live forever.

I'm reminded of a rocket launch where the outer parts of the spaceship fall away and drop back down to earth when they have fulfilled their purpose, while the core of the craft continues upwards to the stars. Paul's saying that we have an outer shell that's burning out and will drop off one day, but all the while, our inner eternal being is actually destined for heaven. Therefore, that's the part that matters to God. That's the part he's intent on refining. That's the part of us that's therefore being perfected and becoming more Christ-like each day, and that's why God will continue to allow us to go through troubles on earth. You see, our refinement is not happening in spite of our troubles here on earth; it's happening *through* our troubles here on earth. Paul says it's exactly our momentary troubles that are achieving for us an eternal glory.

So again, when I get asked, "If God is so good and if Satan is behind all the evil in the world, and if God could stop him at any moment, why does he delay? Why not do it now?" the answer is partly for the same reason he let Abraham wait, and Joseph too, and Moses, and Israel, and David. It's because though Satan means evil for our destruction and it feels unpleasant to us, God is ultimately using it to beautify us and strengthen our souls. In a sense, he's using the power of evil against itself and is bending it to accomplish his own purposes. The Bible says, *"And we know that God causes everything to work together for the good of those who love God and are called according to his purpose for them." (Romans 8:28)* God works all things for good...even evil!

If we're ever tempted to be angry at God for that - for not intervening sooner in world events or cutting short our painful trials, we should remember that he didn't cut short or intervene in his own either! Remember how he let Judas betray him before his crucifixion? This was the greatest evil in history and Jesus knew it was coming. He knew how much atrocious suffering was up ahead for him and yet he didn't try to stop it from happening. Instead, Jesus simply said to Judas, *"Hurry and do what you're going to do." (John 13:27)*

Can we grasp the gravity of that sentence? *"Hurry up and betray me, Judas, who I've loved and taught and cared for these past years. Hurry up and hand me over to have my body whipped and scourged to the point I become so disfigured, I barely look human anymore. Hurry up and get the Roman guards to drive a crown of thorns into my scalp, then hammer iron nails into my wrists and feet as I hang on a cross in the scorching midday sun, feeling my life draining away in the most agonising and excruciating manner mankind has ever devised. Hurry up and do that, Judas."*

Why would Jesus not stand in his way? Because Jesus was going to use evil against itself to accomplish his own purposes! Through his own suffering, he would bring joy to the world. Through his own death, he would bring life. The betrayal wouldn't derail the salvation plan. In fact, it was going to *achieve* the salvation plan. And if God can turn that worst of evils into something good, he can turn whatever we're going through into something good too.

Whatever pain, trial or hardship we're experiencing, if we approach it in the right way, and keep our faith in Jesus throughout, out of a death will always come new life. Problems will in fact turn out to be opportunities. The sad ending of one era will turn out be the exciting beginning of another.

James Stewart wrote about this concept powerfully when he quoted Psalm 68:18 saying, *"It is a glorious phrase - 'He led captivity captive.' The very triumphs of his foes, it means he used for their defeat. He compelled their dark achievements to subserve his end, not theirs. They nailed him to a tree, not knowing that by that very act they were bringing the world to his feet. They gave him a cross, not guessing that he would make it a throne. They flung him outside the city gates to die, not knowing that in that very moment they were lifting up the gates of the universe, to let the king come in. They thought to root out his doctrines, not understanding that they were implanting imperishably in the hearts of men the very name they intended to destroy. They thought they had God with his back to the wall, pinned helpless and defeated: they did not know that it was God himself who had tracked them down. He did not conquer in spite of the dark mystery of evil. He conquered through it."*[5]

We Hope

When not even death has any power over us, what is there left to fear? Nothing. Therefore, we shouldn't be like the world, scared of the future and scrambling to escape it by running back to our youth. Neither should we become too wistful for the places we've already been. There are much greater things ahead! Indeed, we should look forward with bold and confident expectation.

It's interesting to note the contrasting attitudes towards death in the Bible, pre-Jesus and post-Jesus. In the Old Testament, before Jesus had come to conquer death and offer the world hope, King Hezekiah was told by God that he was going to die. The Bible says, *"About that time Hezekiah became deathly ill, and the prophet Isaiah son of Amoz went to visit him. He gave the king this message: 'This is what the Lord says: Set your affairs in order, for you are going to die. You will not recover from this illness."* (2 Kings 20:1) The Bible explains how Hezekiah then *"broke down and wept bitterly."* Hezekiah was absolutely shattered by the news his life was ending and he pleaded with God to be given more time.

Fast forward to the New Testament though, after Jesus had conquered death, and you find his followers treating it with a kind of casual disdain that even we may find surprising! Remember Paul wrote, *"To live is Christ and to die is gain...I'm torn between two desires: I long to go and be with Christ, which would be far better for me. But for your sakes, it is better that I continue to live."* (Philippians 1:21,23-24) He's seemingly quite eager to be done with the wilderness and to go home to the promised land! To the Corinthians he also mocked death saying things like, *"O death, where is your victory? O death, where is your sting?"* (1 Corinthians 15:55) He's almost dancing on the grave of death with that statement. It holds no fear for him whatsoever. He *wants* to go home.

And then we read about the first Christian martyr, Stephen. As his killers picked up stones to pelt him to death, Stephen demonstrated a serenity that baffled and almost scared them. The Bible says, *"Stephen, full of the Holy Spirit, gazed steadily into heaven and saw the glory of God, and he saw Jesus standing in the place of honour at God's right hand. And he told them, "Look, I see the heavens opened and the Son of Man standing in the place of honour at God's right hand!"* Even as the rocks began to shatter his bones and the blood began to pour from his wounds, Stephen seemed pleased to be going to his Saviour. The Bible reports that he simply said, *"'Lord Jesus, receive my spirit.' He fell to his knees, shouting, 'Lord, don't charge them with this sin!'" (Acts 7: 54-60)* Not only did Stephen go serenely to his death in a manner that proved he just wasn't scared of it anymore, he made sure that his killers were forgiven for it. What a beautiful soul! So very Christ-like. He was clearly refined and ready to go home.

So let's all be like Paul and Stephen in this respect, rather than like Hezekiah. Let's all be fearless in life *and* in death, because we know where we're going. For the Christian, whatever doesn't kill you makes you stronger, and whatever does kill you simply sends you home.[6]

I'm actually reminded of when my Grandma was dying here. I'm not exactly sure what was wrong with her as I was still quite young, but it wasn't a quick death - she was in a hospital bed for quite a while as far as I remember. In her final hours, my parents went to visit her one last time. Everyone knew the end was in sight and could come at any moment so it was thought best that me and my siblings shouldn't be there just in case we witnessed something distressing. But I remember my parents coming home from that final hospital visit and my mum reporting something very strange: Grandma had sounded *excited*. She was a firm believer in Christ, had lived a long life, had lost her husband around fifteen years beforehand, and the thought of going home to see him, and her Saviour, and to be free of her failing body, had left her feeling...*excited*. It was as though she'd been waiting for this very moment all her life. The promised land was just moments away. In fact, I believe her last words to my parents were something along the lines of, "I want to go home! I want to go home!"

For me as a young child who thought the world was brilliant and so full of wonder, I couldn't understand why anyone would want to leave it so willingly at the time. But now as an adult, I do understand what she meant - it actually wasn't such a strange reaction after all. Indeed, I now hope that when we each reach our own final breaths, we're all equally excited to go see our Saviour, equally confident in what comes next, and that we remember that what we're leaving behind is only a wilderness by comparison.

We Have Work To Do

In the meantime, let's not forget that we have work to do! I keep coming back to this. It would be easy to see the decay in the world, contrast it with the glory of the world to come, abandon this wilderness to its fate, and simply wait for God to get us out of here. But we know that's not what this is all about. As long as you have breath in your body, you have work to do. You're here for a purpose. Remember, *"For we are God's masterpiece. He created us anew in Christ Jesus, so we can do the good things he planned for us long ago." (Ephesians 2:10)* God has planned for you to do something here, and through it, not only will you change reality in some way, your own soul will be purified in the process. It doesn't matter how old you are either. You're never too old to start pursuing a new vision and living the life you should.

Again, I must say this: Don't let life happen to you; make sure you happen to life! Do something with it that matters. The meaning of life is threefold: Love God, love others, and live in a worthy cause. Now that we understand how dark and futile life is for the unbeliever, shouldn't we try to tell them about Jesus all the more? Shouldn't we, with the greatest urgency, share the hope and meaning we've found? And shouldn't we do it fearlessly too, knowing that the world can actually do nothing to us in response? So what if we perish in the attempt? We'll close our eyes in this world and open them a second later in the next!

However we go about making an impact here, just know that it *matters*. Just know that *you* matter. Whatever you do in life may feel small or insignificant at the time but it's not. Everything matters. Your tiny act of obedience can have a domino effect that echoes throughout eternity. Indeed, every offering you put forward for God's kingdom matters *forever*. And so do you. That's why Jesus gave up his life for you.

And don't be discouraged by the circumstances either. Yes, the world is slowly unravelling and it will continue to do so, but even within that context of decay, we can still bring life. Like Wiberforce, Wallace, Luther King Jr., the Wright Brothers et al., if we forget about the obstacles and just try, reality can be beaten. Even the laws of Physics can be beaten through the power of Jesus! Didn't Peter walking on the water teach us that very thing? Therefore have faith in what Jesus can do through you. He doesn't ask you to do everything. He doesn't ask you to save the entire world...he already took care of that. You just need to do the thing he put you here to do. You just need to make a difference in whatever way you can. Even if you just have two mites in your pocket, throw them in. Be obedient and you can make a difference.

There's a famous story along these lines that goes like this: *"Once upon a time, there was a wise man who used to go to the ocean to do his writing. He had a habit of walking on the beach before he began his work.*

One day, as he was walking along the shore, he looked down the beach and saw a human figure moving like a dancer. He smiled to himself at the thought of someone who would dance to the day, and so, he walked faster to catch up.

As he got closer, he noticed that the figure was that of a young man, and that what he was doing was not dancing at all. The young man was reaching down to the shore, picking up small objects, and throwing them into the ocean.

He came closer still and called out "Good morning! May I ask what it is that you are doing?" The young man paused, looked up, and replied, "Throwing starfish into the ocean."

"I must ask, then, why are you throwing starfish into the ocean?" asked the somewhat startled wise man. To this the young man replied, "The sun is up and the tide is going out. If I don't throw them in, they'll die."

Upon hearing this, the wise man commented, "But young man, do you not realise that there are miles and miles of beach and there are thousands of starfish all along every mile? You can't possible make a difference!" At this, the young man bent down, picked up yet another starfish, and threw it into the ocean. As it met the water, he said, "It made a difference for that one."

The young, idealistic man reminded the older, perhaps slightly more cynical man, of a truth that he seemed to have forgotten: that just because he is only one person and can't do *everything*, that shouldn't preclude him from doing the something he *can* do. Let's learn the lesson from that story, and let's all of us do something. Little is much when God is in it.

Sanctification

And finally, since our souls are eternal and are being prepared for the moment we finally go home, let's be intentional about cultivating beauty and strength in them.

When I was growing up I used to love watching the TV sit-com, *Friends*. The series ran from 1994 to 2004, and it was literally just about six friends who were doing life together in their twenties - they were in the part of life where they were getting their own apartments for the first time, searching for jobs, dating and trying to find their niche in the world.

I was such an avid watcher of Friends that I saw all the episodes multiple times over and could quote the lines by heart. The storylines became so entrenched in my mind, and indeed the minds of most of my generation, that we could relate to each other through the storylines. For example, when I was a teenager I tried to grow my hair long and at my cousin's wedding, the heat and humidity caused it to get a bit unruly. When I was talking to my friends about it, all I had to say was that my hair had "done a Monica", they would instantly know what that meant.

Around my mid twenties, the syndication rights for Friends in the UK were sold to a channel I didn't have access to, so from that moment, the show faded from my life. It's not that I didn't want to watch it - it's just that it wasn't there anymore, and I didn't own any of the DVDs.

Many years later, having not seen a single episode for a long time, I was flicking through the channels when I happened to see that Friends was showing again, and I was curious and quite excited to watch it. I wondered if I'd still enjoy it as much, if it had dated, and if it had retained the old charm that I remembered from long ago.

Well, within five minutes I was actually quite repelled...almost every single joke during that time was centred on sex, or sexual organs, or gay innuendos. Furthermore, the conversations between the characters had never once moved beyond who was having sex, and with whom, and who wasn't having sex, and why they weren't having sex, and how they were determined to start having sex again...had it always been this smutty?! In my memory, I was sure they sometimes talked about other things. But now I wasn't so sure! I found myself uncomfortable with it in a way I never had been in the past.

The morality of the episode wasn't helping either. It was an episode where one of the main characters, Chandler, is chatting to an anonymous woman online. Things take a romantic twist and Chandler thinks he might like to meet this woman in real life and get to know her better. Unfortunately, the woman then drops the bomb that she is already married. Upon hearing this information, Chandler, quite rightly, backs away from the relationship and stops responding to her messages. So far so good.

However, that's only until Phoebe hears about it. Phoebe, another of the main characters, can't believe Chandler is about to give up on this woman. Phoebe is a kind of New Age hippy and she says something like, "What if this woman isn't meant to be with her husband, Chandler? What if she's meant to be with you?" In other words, "what if the 'Universe' wants you to commit adultery with this woman, cause emotional devastation, break up her marriage with her husband, and potentially ruin the family life of their kids? What if the universe wants that, Chandler? What if?"

This is enough to convince Chandler. He starts talking to the woman again and they meet up in person. And the strange thing is that because the audience knows Chandler, likes Chandler and wants Chandler to be happy, and because they don't know this other faceless husband guy, they find themselves rooting for Chandler. The audience actually starts rooting for the adultery!

I was extremely uncomfortable. It was though I was seeing the whole show through a new set of eyes and I didn't really want to watch it anymore. It still undeniably had funny lines and relatable moments, but overriding it all was a sense that this was somehow corrupting for the soul. The eternal part of me that is destined to go on to the new earth was being blackened by this experience.

Whenever I think about entertainment and the way it helps or hinders the sanctification of our soul, I always think again of what Paul wrote to the Philippians: *"Fix your thoughts on what is true, and honourable, and right, and pure, and lovely, and admirable. Think about things that are excellent and worthy of praise." (Philippians 4:8)* I found that this episode of Friends had none of those qualities and that it bothered me in a way it never had before.

And this is what sanctification looks like. As we walk through life, we should each have similar experiences. We should each discover someday that we hate things that we used to love, and we love things we used to hate, because our souls are being remade in the image of Jesus, and we are being refined for citizenship of our eternal home.

When we get home incidentally and the old body has fallen away, what's left, who we are inside, will be a reflection of who we worshipped throughout life. For whatever we worship, we are becoming. So the question is, what matters the most to you? What's your ultimate goal in life? How does that reflect in the person you're becoming? How does that reflect in what entertains you?

There's an old Graham Kendrick song that says, *"All I once held dear, built my life upon, all this world reveres and wars to own, all I once thought gain I have counted loss, Spent and worthless now compared to this...knowing Jesus."* That pretty much sums it up. If we're looking at life in the right way, Jesus is now all that matters. Because it's only through him that life matters at all. Therefore, the best thing we can do is prepare ourselves to meet him.

Chapter Eight

Going Home

"The pain that you have been feeling cannot compare to the joy that is coming." (Romans 8:18)

In Scotland our winters can be particularly harsh. As I write in late December the shortest day of the year has just passed and the sun set at around 3:30pm this afternoon. That is early!

In fact, it can be so dark and cold during these winter months, and they can seem to last for so long, that by the time February comes around, summer almost starts to feel like a lie. It's almost like you start to doubt your own memory that tells you it once really existed. You forget what it was like to step outside the front door and not feel your bones being chilled by the frigid air. You forget what it's like not to have to wrap up in five layers just to get groceries, or to have to set aside extra time whenever you go anywhere because the car needs to defrost. You forget too, what it's like not to live under seemingly perpetual darkness. In a sense, the present reality starts to argue strongly that it's the only kind of reality there is. And the longer you're in it, the more you start to believe the argument. You begin to doubt whether you'll ever see a warm day again, and you lose memory of just how that might feel.

Living a long life on a corrupted earth can have a similar impact on us. We each had a glimpse of Eden in our childhoods but almost instantly our naivety began to unravel. And the further away we get from those early days of hope and optimism, the more we experience of life's persistent, cold, dark chaos, the more we can start to doubt our own memory. Did we *really* feel so excited about life as a child? Were we *really* that joyful? What exactly *did* that feel like? We may not truly remember anymore. And what's more, we may even start to doubt that a place could possibly exist that would fulfil those longings. What I mean is, we may begin to doubt that a reality other than this one can actually be true. Of course, we can read the Bible and hear the promises of how wonderful heaven will be, but even so, there's a risk we'll eventually succumb to cynicism.

Remember what happened when Abraham and Sarah had to wait a long time for Isaac? Doubt started to creep in that God was going to stay true to his promise and they tried to force the issue with Hagar. Remember how long Israel had to wait in the wilderness? Forty years. They waited so long that many of them started to grumble and doubt whether there was a promised land ahead for them at all. Furthermore, they were sceptical about whether any promised land could possibly be worth all the current pain. Many of them just wanted to turn back and return to slavery in Egypt.

So when the Bible tells us that Jesus is going to delay his second coming for a very long time, we should be unsurprised to find many beginning to doubt that he's coming back at all. Peter says, "*...in the last days scoffers will come, mocking the truth and following their own desires. They will say, 'What happened* to the promise Jesus is coming again? From before the times of our ancestors, everything has remained the same since the world was first created.'" (1 Peter 3:3-4) The longer people live in the darkness, the more likely they are to be sceptical of the existence of light.

Furthermore, because the present suffering will only get worse over time, a great swathe of the church will even lose heart and fall away from the faith. Paul writes about the tribulation of the end times saying, "For [the return of Christ] will not come, except there come a falling away first..." (2 Thessalonians 2:3) (KJV) Jesus himself says, "Sin will be rampant everywhere, and the love of many will grow cold." (Matthew 24:12) Jesus also rhetorically implies that there will be little faith on the earth by the time of his return when he says, "When the Son of Man returns, how many will he find on the earth who have faith?" (Luke 18:8)

So when people lose heart due to a long, hard wait, the Bible says they will lose **hope** that Jesus is coming back at all. That means that they'll fall away from the **faith**. And furthermore, Jesus says their **love** will grow cold. And what three things are we told must last forever into eternity? "Three things will last forever - faith, hope, and love - and the greatest of these is love." (1 Corinthians 13:13) Faith saves us, hope sustains us and to love God and others is the meaning of life itself. Therefore, when we understand it all depends on not losing heart, we can understand why we are implored to stay strong in the midst of trials. Indeed, Jesus warned his disciples of the struggles they would experience and then said, "I have told you these things so that you may have peace in me. Here on *earth you will have many trials and sorrows. But take heart,* *because I have overcome the world." (John 16:33)*

Take heart! Elsewhere in the Bible we read, *"Therefore we do not lose heart..." (2 Corinthians 4:16), "Let us not become weary..." (Galatians 6:9), "Be strong and let your heart take courage..." (Psalm 31:24)* Take heart! Take heart! Take heart! Jesus is effectively looking us deep in the eye through his word and saying, "Look, I'm going away for a long time and I'm not going to lie, life is going to be difficult until I get back. But listen to me now...you *must* listen to me: Do *not* worry. Do *not* be afraid. Do *not* lose heart...I've got this. I *will* come back to get you. This *will* all make sense one day. Trust me."

To "take" heart implies being intentional. Heart doesn't just come to you, you've got to reach out and take it. Indeed, in a broken world, it's the other things that will come to you - scepticism comes to you, cynicism comes to you, bitterness comes to you. And as those things infect your heart, it'll make your soul sick unto death. Why? Because when your **faith** turns to scepticism, when your **hope** turns to cynicism and when your **love** turns to bitterness, you are dying inside. You have nothing to save you, nothing to sustain you, and nothing to make your life worthwhile. That's why Satan wages war on our souls in this way. He knows that if our hearts are defeated, we will be ruined inside long, long before the Second Law of Thermodynamics claims our bodies.

Remember again what Solomon wrote about the potential for a long delay to make our hearts sick: *"Hope deferred makes the heart sick." (Proverbs 13:12)* And we simply can't let it happen to us. Take heart! Yes, we have to actively take it, and pursue that which nourishes our souls.

Looking Ahead To Glory

One of the primary ways in which we can take heart is to look forward to the New Earth in anticipation. Paul gives us a vague but exciting insight into it when he says, *"Yet what we suffer now is nothing compared to the glory he will reveal to us later. For all creation is waiting eagerly for that future day when God will reveal who his children really are. Against its will, all creation was subjected to God's curse. But with eager hope, the creation looks forward to the day when it will join God's children in glorious freedom from death and decay." (Romans 8:18-21)*

I'm always struck by what a bold claim this is from Paul. I mean, think about the sufferings we go through here. Think about bone cancer, and mutilation, and beheadings, and sexual abuse, and all the most disgusting struggles that people actually face. That will appear as *nothing* compared to the glory of what's to come?! That's a *massive* claim!

But Paul isn't downplaying or trivialising the pain we feel by that statement - in other parts of the Bible he demonstrates a clear and articulate understanding of acute suffering. He's not naive and he's certainly not one to be flippant about pain either. Therefore, if he's *still* willing to make the claim that it will all appear as nothing compared to the glory to come, we can only conclude that the glory to come will be glorious beyond comprehension!

I guess it's a bit like a boxer who punishes his body for months to get himself into top condition for a big fight. Every morning he's awake at 5am to go jogging on cold, dark streets. He runs until his legs are collapsing from underneath him and his lungs are ready to burst. He trains in the gym until his muscles tremble and ache. He eats a heavily restricted diet and avoids all the good things he would like to enjoy, gritting his teeth in all circumstances to beat his own body into submission. Indeed, it's such a gruelling schedule that he hates every second of it. And yet the moment he's crowned champion, somehow all of that fades away from his memory. He can barely even remember what the pain of the training felt like - it's just completely overwhelmed and subdued by the elation of the victory, and he knows it was all worth it. Muhammad Ali famously said about this, *"I hated every minute of training, but I said, 'Don't quit. Suffer now and live the rest of your life as a champion.'"*[1]

An even better illustration would be childbirth. To my mind (and except for man-flu obviously), childbirth looks like the most painful experience on earth. There are screams of agony. There's blood, sweat and tears. And it lasts for hours! To all intents and purposes, the experience looks absolutely horrific. I'm sure when the mother is in the moment, it seems like nothing could be worth that pain. And yet just a little while later, when she's holding the newborn baby in her arms, the elation is so overwhelming that she'd be more than willing to go through it all again. So indeed, after one child often comes another, and possibly another. It's like the joy of holding the child has undone the memory of the pain in some way.

I think these are small examples of what Paul is getting at. The glory of the New Earth is going to be so staggering, so outrageously overwhelming, that there's no pain on this earth that it won't subdue, and even undo. The worst discomforts will seem trivial when compared to the glory of heaven, and we'll know that it was all worth it.

In order to reach that final goal, we only need to fix our eyes on it and go - holding onto faith, hope and love at all times. When life hits, we get up. When life hits harder, we get up stronger. When life beats us down a hundred times, we get up a hundred-and-one times. Life ain't about how hard you can hit. It's about how hard you can get hit and keep moving forward. How much you can take and keep moving forward. That's how winning is done!

The Bible tells us that if we persevere through all circumstances like this, we will be called winners for Christ! Indeed the Bible uses the term "overcomer" or "victor". There's a lot of talk about overcomers in Revelation, and the rewards are high: *"To everyone who is victorious I will give fruit from the tree of life in the paradise of God." (Revelation 2:7) "Whoever is victorious will not be harmed by the second death." (Revelation 2:11) "To all who are victorious, who obey me to the very end, to them I will give authority over all the nations." (Revelation 2:26) "All who are victorious will be clothed in white. I will never erase their names from the Book of Life, but I will announce before my Father and his angels that they are mine." (Revelation 3:5) "Those who are victorious will sit with me on my throne..." (Revelation 3:21)*

There can often be arguments in Christian circles about whether it's possible to turn away from your salvation and to give it up. Some people think that once you're saved, you're always saved. But I think from these verses and many others, the truth is that it is possible to turn away from Jesus in the face of trials and give up your inheritance. In other words, it *is* possible to have your name erased from the Book of Life. Being a Christian requires perseverance until the very end. This is further confirmed by The Parable of the Sower when Jesus said, *"The seed on the rocky soil represents those who hear the message and immediately receive it with joy. But since they don't have deep roots, they don't last long. They fall away as soon as they have problems or are persecuted for believing God's word."* (*Matthew 13:20-21*) Therefore, the victors the Bible talks about are only those who *endure.*

Indeed, elsewhere in the Bible, Paul encourages us with similar boxing and athletic metaphors about endurance. He says, *"Don't you realise that in a race everyone runs, but only one person gets the prize? So run to win! All athletes are disciplined in their training. They do it to win a prize that will fade away, but we do it for an eternal prize. So I run with purpose in every step. I am not just shadowboxing. I discipline my body like an athlete, training it to do what it should. Otherwise, I fear that after preaching to others I myself might be disqualified."* (*1 Corinthians 9:24-27*)

When we consider that Muhammad Ali was willing to go through the gruelling pain of training to get a temporal prize, how much more should we be willing to persevere when we know our faith will gain us an eternal prize? And notice how Paul also says that he fears he could be "disqualified" if he didn't persevere in the faith? What would disqualify a person from the New Earth? Simply losing heart, thereby losing **hope**, thereby falling away from the **faith**, thereby letting his **love** grow cold. Paul doesn't want that. He wants to stick in despite the struggles, and one day be known as an "overcomer". Hopefully we do too! So we must *take* heart!

But either way, over and over, the Bible confirms that it's only those who persevere in their faith until the very end who will be called "overcomers", and who will gain eternal life. And what the Bible is also keen to stress is that the eternal life will be worth it!

The New Earth In Revelation

Paul vaguely told us that the New Earth would have an immense glory to it, but the Bible actually gives us far more detailed descriptions. Indeed, where Genesis opened by giving us a glimpse into Eden, Revelation concludes by giving us a glimpse into its replacement - the New Earth. And since the revelation comes from Jesus himself we know that this insight is trustworthy and true. It was written down faithfully by John, one of Jesus' disciples, during a period of imprisonment on the isle of Patmos.

Now before we look at it, it's important to say that from this corrupted vantage point, we can't really grasp the full extent of how wonderfully brilliant it will be. Paul confirmed this when he wrote, *"Now we see things imperfectly, like puzzling reflections in a mirror, but then we will see everything with perfect clarity." (1 Corinthians 13:12)* Unfortunately, we just can't help but see the New Earth through a slightly tainted lens, so some of the vision is a little puzzling. Indeed, it seems that John's vocabulary is often stretched to breaking point as he tries to describe it. Nevertheless, it's the clearest insight we have. Therefore John writes, *"Then I saw a new heaven and a new earth, for the old heaven and the old earth had disappeared. And the sea was gone." (Revelation 21:1)*

This first insight establishes that there will indeed be a new earth. That's important because many people, when they think about eternity, have had their mental image distorted by medieval artwork, films, cartoons, television shows and other forms of popular media. In these skewed visions, they have been fed an image of a white, colourless place that is a bit misty, ethereal, and perhaps even ghostly. They imagine the entrance to heaven is a single pearl gate, outside which is Peter, who stands on a cloud wearing robes, and who holds a quill pen in his hand. Before him is a lectern with a guest list, and behind him generally lies more clouds suspended in the air. People often think that anyone who is allowed to pass through heaven's gate by Peter will then spend their days sitting on those clouds playing harps, in a kind of vegetative mental state, staring serenely into the middle distance for all eternity, or singing endless choral songs.

You'll be relieved to hear that none of that is true. The Bible tells us that the New Earth will be every bit as tangible, solid, and real as this one! And we will have real bodies to experience it with too. Paul writes, *"For our dying bodies must be transformed into bodies that will never die; our mortal* bodies must be transformed into immortal bodies." (1 Corinthians 15:53) He also writes, "We, too, wait with eager hope for the day when God will give us our full rights as his adopted children, including the new bodies he promised us." (Romans 8:23)

Christianity is the only faith in the world that teaches that the material body is good. The majority of other religions teach that the material body is bad and the goal of life is to escape them and to live one day only as spirits. I'm glad that's not true either. The truth is that we will one day be given new, incorruptible bodies, and we will be able to see, touch, taste, hear and smell with them just the same as we can now. The only difference of course, is that our senses will be heightened and everything on the New Earth will be even more beautiful and vibrant to behold.

As for the phrase, "And the sea was gone", it could be a literal description and I wouldn't discount that option completely, but there's a fair chance this is prophetic language. In Isaiah 57:20, we read, "Those who reject me are like the restless sea, which is never still but continually churns up mud and dirt." The fact John doesn't notice a sea in his vision of the New Earth is likely to metaphorically mean that there are no wicked, God-rejecting people there.

Let's read on now to see what else was revealed to John: "And I saw the holy city, the new Jerusalem, coming down from God out of heaven like a bride beautifully dressed for her husband. I heard a loud shout from the throne, saying, "Look, God's home is now among his people! He will live with them, and they will be his people. God himself will be with them. He *will wipe every tear from their eyes, and there will be no more death or sorrow or crying or pain. All these things are gone forever." (Revelation 21:2-4)*

This passage primarily tells us that the New Earth will be unified under the rule of God, who will establish his throne in a beautiful capital city called the New Jerusalem. Because God himself is now dwelling among us and reigning over us, the whole world will be at perfect peace, and there will be no suffering there - no tears, no death, no sorrow, no pain. All those things are gone forever.

John continues: *"And the one sitting on the throne said, "Look, I am making everything new!" And then he said to me, "Write this down, for what I tell you is trustworthy and true." And he also said, "It is finished! I am the Alpha and the Omega—the Beginning and the End. To all who are thirsty I will give freely from the springs of the water of life. All who are victorious will inherit all these blessings, and I will be their God, and they will be my children. But cowards, unbelievers, the corrupt, murderers, the immoral, those who practice witchcraft, idol worshipers, and all liars—their fate is in the fiery lake of burning sulphur. This is the second death."* (Revelation 21:5-8)

This passage tells us that sin won't exist on the New Earth. All the evils that were alien to us as children and that took so long for us to adapt to; all those corrupting influences that threatened to induce what Huxley called, a 'mental illness' in us; all the pain that threatened to break our spirits...none of that has any place on the New Earth. It will feel alien to us once again.

This is why we can almost return, in character at least, to the type of people we were in childhood.

Remember Jesus said about children, "the kingdom belongs to such as these." We'll once again experience the kind of raw faith, hope, love and indeed joy that we had in your formative years. And this time, no-one's going to take advantage of us either. We'll be able to leave mobile phones with strangers when we go to the bathroom, and there won't be telesales callers trying to scam us at every turn. Indeed, there will be no sin at all, because all the unreformed and unrepentant sinners have been thrown into the lake of fire. And it's actually interesting that God references childhood in this passage - I don't think it's a mistake. Notice he says that in this sinless world, *"I will be their God and they will be my children."* This is why childhood will always remain so instructive. Glimpse what it means to be a child, and in some small way, you glimpse what it means to be a citizen of the New Earth.

There's a further interesting sub-point in this passage that's worth going off on a tangent to explore: If the New Earth will be sinless, then just how will it be *kept* sinless? I mean, this earth was once perfect too, wasn't it? But Adam and Even used their free-will in Eden to sin and bring about The Fall. Who's to say that won't happen on the New Earth also? As long as people have free-will, won't there always be a risk of *another* Fall?

As far as our free-will goes I can only suggest it will be something like this: Even though I have free-will right now to put my hand in a scorching hot fire, I can tell you that I have absolutely no desire to. None. I am not even slightly tempted to do that. Not a single bit. What's more, I am reasonably certain that for the remainder of my life on earth, I will never develop a desire to put my hand into a scorching fire.

Now what if our desire to sin was like that? What if sin was as appealing as putting my hand in a fire? I think on the New Earth it will be something like that. Whereas our nature here on earth is corrupted and we have therefore inherited a desire for evil, on the New Earth we will have no such desires. Our sanctification - in other words, our transformation into Christ-like beings - will be complete. Therefore, many of our present desires will be completely inverted and we'll only ever have a desire for righteousness.

I think this issue is also another reason why Jesus is delaying his return for so long, and why God is going to allow the world to reach a place of complete degradation before he steps in. You see, it seems that the reason Adam and Eve fell was this: they were ignorant of what would happen when they ate the fruit from the tree of knowledge. Therefore, God has to deal with our ignorance.

It's like this: before this earth was made, God created beings that we'd know as angels. These angels, we believe, lived in a perfectly harmonious society under God's rule, and from the moment they were conceived, they never knew anything else but a pure and peaceful life.

The Bible suggests that one of their number, an angel called Lucifer, one day began to imagine what life apart from God might look like. And the more he thought about it, the more he liked the idea. He imagined that if he came out from under the authority of God, he could become god of his own life and set his own rules. He ruminated on the thought and rebellion continued to grow in his heart. Soon he was sharing his ideas with the other angels and trying to convince them to join him in a revolt.

And here's the thing: because none of the angels had ever experienced life outside of God's authority, none of them knew whether Lucifer's idea was a good one or not. There was an ignorance about the whole thing. So when Lucifer kept spreading the rumour that God was a tyrant and that they'd be better off breaking away, as time went by, some of the angels were swayed. Indeed, eventually around a third of the angels decided to throw their weight behind Lucifer's rebellion, and war broke out in heaven.

Of course, their rebellion failed and they became utterly wretched beings for distrusting God - they were emptied of all goodness and cast out of heaven. But interestingly, the *exact* same thing then happened to human beings. Adam and Eve too were created perfect, set down in a perfect world, and knew nothing of sin. Just like the angels before them. And again, along came Lucifer (now called Satan) into this harmonious setting, and he whispered in their ears the very same lies that he'd whispered to the angels.

He told the man and woman that they could become autonomous beings and live outside the rule of God. He told them that life would be better that way and that they could become their own gods. Like the angels before, ignorance was the problem here. Adam and Eve just don't know if Satan is telling them the truth or not. Maybe life *would* be better without God? Who really knew? So the man and woman fell to the temptation, they rebelled against God, and they too became corrupted beings as a consequence.

Therefore, it seems that unless God allows us to experience the full depths of depravity to which life will plunge without him, there will always be a curiosity inside us that will wonder whether we're getting a raw deal. We'll always be imagining what a fully autonomous life would look like. Therefore, in order to protect the peace of the New Earth forever, it seems God has to deal with our ignorance. He has to show us just what terrible gods we are. He has to step back and let us do our thing, and let us experience the full extent of suffering, disaster, deceit, corruption, societal collapse and inhumanity that flows from that, just so that we'll never be tempted to go that way again.

It will mean that when we're living on the New Earth, should someone come along and start a rumour saying, "Maybe life would be better without God?" there won't be a soul who will be tempted by the idea. We'll turn to that person and say, "You idiot! We had a whole lifetime of that on the old earth and it was terrible! There was terrorism, war, sickness, disease, depression, natural disasters...we've already been there and we're not going back!" We'll have a whole wretched history to look back on and we'll have no desire ever to leave God's kingdom again. That's another reason why we need the wilderness before the promised land.

Let's come back from that tangent and read on to see what else John says about the New Earth now: *"Then one of the seven angels who held the seven bowls containing the seven last plagues came and said to me, "Come with me! I will show you the bride, the wife of the Lamb. So he took me in the Spirit to a great, high mountain, and he showed me the holy city,*

Jerusalem, descending out of heaven from God. It shone with the glory of God and sparkled like a precious stone—like jasper as clear as crystal. The city wall was broad and high, with twelve gates guarded by twelve angels. And the names of the twelve tribes of Israel were written on the gates. There were three gates on each side—east, north, south, and west. The wall of the city had twelve foundation stones, and on them were written the names of the twelve apostles of the Lamb. The angel who talked to me held in his hand a gold measuring stick to measure the city, its gates, and its wall. When he measured it, he found it was a square, as wide as it was long. In fact, its length and width and height were each 1,400 miles. Then he measured the walls and found them to be 216 feet thick (according to the human standard used by the angel)." (Revelation 21:9-17)

There's a lot of continued focus on the New Jerusalem here - the capital city of the New Earth - and we get a bit of insight into how glorious it's going to be. First of all, it's 1,400 square miles, and that's big. Very big! To give a sense of the scale, it would roughly be the size of Indonesia.

John tries to convey its glory by comparing it to jewels but I think this is an example of his vocabulary being stretched to breaking point. Even if we picture jasper and crystal I still don't think we're really getting close to it. It will be glorious though. More glorious than we can imagine.

The fact it's a cube is symbolic because in the Old Testament the part of the Temple where God resided was a cube shaped room called the Holy of Holies. Therefore, the fact the whole city is represented as a cube may be taken as metaphor for the fact that the whole place will now be considered the Holy of Holies i.e. the place where God himself dwells and has his throne. This is further alluded to when we read on:

"I saw no temple in the city, for the Lord God Almighty and the Lamb are its temple. And the city has no need of sun or moon, for the glory of God illuminates the city, and the Lamb is its light. The nations will walk in its light, and the kings of the world will enter the city in all their glory. Its gates will never be closed at the end of day because there is no night there. And all the nations will bring their glory and honour into the city. Nothing evil will be allowed to enter, nor anyone who practices shameful idolatry and dishonesty—but only those whose names are written in the Lamb's Book of Life." (Revelation 21:22-27)

So there won't be a temple because God himself is dwelling amongst his people. Therefore, the whole city becomes the Holy of Holies.

It's also worth noticing from this passage that Jerusalem won't be the only city on the New Earth. When it says "the nations will walk in its light", it's telling us that the rest of the world will be divided into nations, just like today. We're not given any insight into what the nations will look like but since he made this world to be extremely diverse, it's fair to assume that the New Earth will be even more so. The great thing about Christianity is that it doesn't demand cultural conformity. If you go to an African church, a Western church and then an Asian church, you're going to see different types of dress, styles of worship and skin colours, and all of it is pleasing to God. I imagine the New Earth will be something quite similar.

Very importantly however, we're told that these nations will have kings ruling over them, and that the kings will make visits to Jerusalem "in all their glory." Who are these kings? Well...maybe you! Remember what Revelation said earlier: *"To all who are victorious, who obey me to the very end, to them I will give authority over all the nations." (Revelation 2:26)*

The Bible tells us that Jesus will rule over the New Earth but that we, as his bride, will be co-heirs in that inheritance. In other words, he will delegate authority to us so that we join in his rulership. This is another reason why we have to go through some trials here, and it's another way in which God is bending evil for his own good, eternal purposes. Therefore Paul wrote, *"If we endure hardship, we will reign with him." (2 Timothy 2:12)* He also writes, *"And since we are his children, we are his heirs. In fact, together with Christ, we are heirs of God's glory. But if we are to share in his glory, we must also share in his suffering." (Romans 8:17)*

In Luke 19, Jesus tells the Parable of the Ten Servants to confirm this idea. The parable describes a ruler who leaves a little money with his ten servants while he goes away for a long time to be crowned king. When he returns, he wants a report from each of the servants on how they have used what was given to them. To the ones who have done well, he delegates to them some of his authority and makes them rulers over cities: *"'Well done!' the king exclaimed. 'You are a good servant. You have been faithful with the little I entrusted you, so you will be governor of ten cities as your reward.'" (Luke 19:17)*

In the parable, the master represents Jesus. He has gone away for a long time but he has left his servants the Holy Spirit and the instruction to do good work for his kingdom. Soon he is coming back as the King of kings, and when he returns he's going to want a report of what we did in his absence. Have we been faithful? Have we worked hard for his kingdom and for his name's sake? Have we kept persevering in the face of suffering? If we have stayed faithful despite all the trials and tribulations, he will make us co-heirs, we will be crowned, and we will be given responsibility to rule over a portion of his eternal kingdom.

Therefore, when Revelation talks about kings coming and going from the New Jerusalem, it really might be talking about you! That's no exaggeration. We are princes and princesses here training to be kings and queens of the New Earth. And clearly from John's vision, we will need to come to Jesus in the New Jerusalem occasionally to run some ideas past him!

I guess this is an obvious point but I should say that this means we're not all going to be living in the New Jerusalem. I think sometimes we believe heaven is a very concentrated area and we'll all be piled into the one place. But actually, there's a whole planet with many nations to live in, just like there is right now. Therefore, whether you want your house to be by a lake, in a forest, in the mountains, or whether you're a city dweller and want an apartment in a skyscraper, you'll be able to live wherever you choose.

Let's read on again: *"Then the angel showed me a river with the water of life, clear as crystal, flowing from the throne of God and of the Lamb. It flowed down the centre of the main street. On each side of the river grew a tree of life, bearing twelve crops of fruit, with a fresh crop each month. The leaves were used for medicine to heal the nations." (Revelation 22:1-2)*

When I think of this passage, I get an image in my mind of the Lincoln Memorial in Washington DC, the capital city of the United States. If you've ever been there, there's a huge building, almost like a temple, that houses a giant statue of the former US President, Abraham Lincoln. Immediately below it there's a long thin man-made lake with parkland trees either side. God's throne in the New Jerusalem is obviously going to look far more spectacular than that, and there will be a clear river flowing out of it rather than a lake, but it perhaps gives some idea of the configuration.

There's more to this passage than perhaps meets the eye. For example, when John describes "twelve crops of fruit, with a fresh crop each month", in a very indirect way, that tells us that time on the New Earth will still be divided into twelve month years, like this earth. And that also suggests there will still be seasons there. Furthermore, it tells us that there will be food on the new earth. Certainly fruit. And that confirms that with our real, literal, physical bodies, we'll still be able to enjoy things with our senses. In other words, we'll still be able to eat!

The food on the New Earth will be pretty exciting too! If you think you've tasted some good food here, just wait till you try the food there. Everything on this earth has been affected by the curse of The Fall. That means the fruit we eat, as good as it is, is a shadow of what it was originally designed to be - it too has been subject to the Second Law of Thermodynamics. Therefore, when everything is restored to glory, it's fair to say that you'll never have tasted anything like it. The peaches, the strawberries, the watermelon, the pears and the oranges will dazzle you in such a way that you'll realise you're only really tasting these things for the first time. Not only that, but since our bodies will be perfect, our tastebuds will be perfectly tuned. So the food itself won't only be juicier, more flavoursome and more sweet, but we'll be better able to appreciate it.

God is good. If ever we're tempted to underestimate the New Earth, we need to remember that. I'm struck by the fact that even on this earth, for every sense we've been given to experience the world with, the Lord has provided some kind of beauty to go with it. For our eyes, we've been given beautiful landscapes and colours. For our ears, we've been given music and birdsong. For our sense of smell we've been given fragrant flowers and other pleasant aromas. For our sense of touch, we've been given hugs, kisses and even sex. For our sense of taste, we've been given delicious food of every kind. There are no materialistic reasons why any of this should be so. What I mean is, there is no evolutionary reason why the world should have been created beautiful. Things have simply been designed this way because God is an artist and he loves us.

And these are just a few examples of the beauty in the world. Therefore, since we know that God wants to lavish us with good things, we can expect even more beauty on the New Earth. We'll be able to do all this in perfect health too: the river of life and the medicines from the trees represent the fact we will all be kept in perfect health forever.

Next passage: *"No longer will there be a curse upon anything. For the throne of God and of the Lamb will be there, and his servants will worship him. And they will see his face, and his name will be written on their foreheads. And there will be no night there—no need for lamps or sun—for the Lord God*

will shine on them. And they will reign forever and ever."
(Revelation 22:3-5)

The curse that God placed on the earth back in Genesis was the moment that the Second Law of Thermodynamics kicked in, and that meant that everything suddenly became difficult to achieve. We were always working against the natural flow of the universe, trying to overcome it to sustain order, even as it tended towards chaos. We had to work and toil to make the ground fruitful, for example, and it always felt like an uphill battle. Often those battles were futile and we had no chance of winning them.

But that's all gone now. The universe no longer tends towards chaos and we no longer have to toil to keep everything in good shape. Furthermore, everything we do is imbued with meaning and our work will be pleasant.

The New Earth Is More

That's about all Revelation gives us regarding the New Earth, but are there any further ways in which we can find encouragement about what's to come? Are there any more ways of looking at eternity that will spur us on to keep the faith? Well, I think we may be able to get a little bit more insight into the New Earth if we remember what this old earth was *originally* created to be.

Remember that when God designed this planet with fresh life-giving rivers, sparkling and tumbling into aquamarine seas that teemed with fish and other forms of marine life; when he designed lush forests and grasslands brimming with animals of every kind; when he designed the soil to produce abundant vegetation and food for all to eat; when he decided there should be snow-peaked mountains and white sandy beaches beyond; and when he created birds flying through skies lit by sun, moon and stars; when he decided the air should be fresh and the planet should be full of vibrant colour...that he pronounced the whole thing was very *good*.

This tells us that God has great aesthetic taste and that we can trust his design! Furthermore, if God created all those things in the first place and thought they were very good, we can likely deduce that the New Earth will not be anything *less* than that. Again, we tend to struggle with this concept because we're used to the pop culture vision of eternity as a white, misty, ethereal, choir service. In other words, we take this earth as our starting point for what it might be like, and then *subtract* goodness from it.

Therefore in our vision of the New Earth, we move from colour to monochrome; from clarity to cloudiness; from tangibility to intangibility; and we end up with something not very appealing. And it really is unappealing. When presented with that kind of vision, we may prefer it to the only other alternative, which is hell, but if we're honest we'd rather not spend eternity in either of them! So the great news here is that we don't have to. That's not what God has planned for us.

Indeed, if we flip our thinking around we'll get much closer to the truth. What I mean is, if we're to use this earth as a starting point for our vision of eternity, we'd do better not to subtract from what we know here, but rather to *add* to what we know here - to try to catch glimpses of original glory through what surrounds us even now. If we do that we'll at least tune our minds in the right way to understand that the New Earth will not be anything less than this one; it will only be something more. It will somehow be *more* colourful, *more* vibrant, and even more *real*. Therefore, try to imagine this world with all the decay undone, and with even more glory besides. Then you may be getting close to a picture of the New Earth. Still not very close. But closer at least.

I remember on one of my road trips into the Scottish countryside a few years ago, I decided to venture off the beaten track into a remote area - in fact it was so far off the beaten track that I can only vaguely remember how to get back there now - but when I arrived I found myself all alone in the middle of a quiet forest.

It was around the middle of summer, and as I walked through the scene, I was taken aback by just how beautiful it was. There was a wide avenue of trees in the forest that opened out into a clearing. The sun was high in a clear blue sky and in this open space, a woodland floor carpeted by lush green grass was being bathed in sunlight. Around the periphery of the clearing, where the trees were slightly more densely packed, there were only shafts of light that flickered with the rhythm of the trees as their leaves swayed in the breeze. And then on the floor, lavishly scattered like confetti, there were flowers of different kinds, and in a dazzling array of colours too - from purples to yellows, whites and blues.

It was like something out of a Disney movie. I felt privileged to have found such an incredible place, and the sense of wonder was only heightened by the fact of knowing that no-one else was ever likely to come this way, or see its glory again. I decided therefore, that I shouldn't rush on by, but rather spend time being intentional about slowing down and appreciating what God had made here. It actually evoked a desire to worship in my heart - I couldn't help but want to thank him for pouring out his goodness on us.

I think when you see something like that, there's really no other appropriate response. Grass, flowers, trees, sunshine and blue skies are things that we sometimes become numb to through familiarity, but if we'd just take a moment to appreciate what God's done with them, I believe we would be stunned by them anew every time.

So there I was. I sat down in the middle of this forest and I decided to look, I mean really look, for the first time in a long time. I examined the way the individual blades of grass were constructed. I held up a flower to the sunlight and saw the intricate craftsmanship within the petals. I looked at pine cones and examined the genius design of spiders webs.

I almost felt a sense of urgency come over me as I looked. Like this was too good to be hidden, and that everyone else in the world should come see it and marvel at it. It deserved to be in a public space where it could be enjoyed and appreciated like a work of art before it disappeared for the winter. It was more beautiful than anything in any art gallery. And yet here it all was tucked away in the middle of nowhere in a place where it's most likely never seen by human eyes at all.

And then it struck me that this exact same spectacle must explode into life *every* year, and that there must be millions of others just like them all over the world, passing by completely unknown and unappreciated. And then it struck me just how wasteful God has been with his goodness. He's been overgenerous really. Outrageously extravagant. That's what this was - outrageously extravagant beauty. The world today, even after thousands of years of unravelling, is still brim-full and spilling over with breath-taking wonders. So what must it have been like *before* all the unravelling began?!

And then I remembered that if God loved us enough to create a planet this wonderful, and if this is just a foreshadow of what's to come, then I could rightly be extremely excited about the kind of world we're going to live on when it's time to go home. That's what the best of this world should evoke in us - a sense of excitement for the one to come.

Therefore, for our own faith's sake, and so that we'll find our souls nourished in the process - so that we'll even learn how be intentional about taking heart - I'd encourage everyone to keep seeking out beauty here. Because it still exists. Actively look for new experiences. Choose to see, draw close, and feel. Rediscover what it means to be a happy wanderer - what it felt like to be that child who would poke, prod, taste and explore. We begin to die inside when we lose our sense of wonder and our faith is recharged when we actively seek it out. It really is often as simple as going for a walk in the countryside too. Or trying a new recipe for dinner, reading a book by a different author, listening to a new kind of music, and it's simply understanding that these are all dim reflections of the joy to come. If you're in a rut, always doing the same things, day after day, just do something different, and you'll be surprised at what your eyes are opened to, and how it gives your soul a lift.

It's All We've Ever Wanted

We're nearly finished now. And all I want to leave you with is the understanding that home is what we've been craving this whole time. Indeed, home is all we've ever really wanted.

In Chapter One, we saw that it's what we wanted when we were kids and we imagined a life of eternal bliss.

In Chapter Two, we saw that it's what parents are trying to keep alive in the hearts of their tweenagers.

In Chapter Three, we saw that home is what we grieved for when the teenage years came around and reality began to beat us down.

In Chapter Four, we saw it's what we look to as we live as ambassadors of Christ on this earth.

In Chapter Five, we saw that a vision of home is the root of the visionary idealism that's in our hearts in young adulthood, and that inspires us to change realities.

In Chapter Six, we saw that home is what we're trying to reach out for in adulthood with all our coping mechanisms and it's where we escape to in our imaginations when we need to recharge our souls. Furthermore, we saw that home is what mankind is constantly trying to resuscitate via The System.

In Chapter Seven, we saw that home is what we look forward to as we're growing old and it's what our souls are being sanctified for through all our struggles and heartaches.

And finally, here in Chapter Eight, we see that home is the place where all our longings will be fulfilled.

CS Lewis said, *"There have been times when I think we do not desire heaven; but more often I find myself wondering whether, in our heart of hearts, we have ever desired anything else."*[2] How true that is. Whether we realise it or not, all of our thoughts, words and deeds throughout life ultimately reveal within us a desperate desire to go home.

Incidentally, this explains why history is so littered with politicians, dictators, social engineers, scientists, science-fiction writers and others trying to find ways to create Utopia on earth. The hiraeth in their hearts for home causes unbelievers to take misguided steps to try to establish it outside the authority of Jesus Christ. Some thought Utopia could be established on earth through Communism. Some thought it could be achieved through Fascism. Some tried eugenics. Others tried concentration camps. Others tried genocides. A dream of building a global Utopia is what also currently drives the development of a One World Order and One World Religion.

All of these fumbling efforts are doomed to failure in the end. In fact, they will only make things worse. They are "Ishmaels". The truth is we will only see the place we long for when we see the place that Jesus himself has made for us.

It's only through him that any of us will get there too. He's delaying his return and it's going to need perseverance to push through, but because of him, everything that takes place here is now just a precursor to our real lives. If you're a Christian, even if you turn 100 years-old on your next birthday, you haven't yet really begun. There's an eternity ahead of you that will be everything you imagined it to be and more. On the day you get there, a heavy weight will drop off your shoulders - a weight you perhaps didn't even realise you were carrying. You'll never want to sleep again because reality will finally be better than your dreams. And you'll live in endless wonder.

The threefold meaning of life will be restored there. You'll be in perfect harmony with God and you'll know him as your loving Father. You'll know Jesus personally and as you walk the streets of the New Jerusalem, you'll see him who died for you in the flesh. You'll have close friendships there and you'll know what it is to love each other perfectly for the first time. You'll go to friend's houses for dinner and you'll have fun. You'll hang by the pool, tell stories and eat good food. You'll have real bodies with which to enjoy life too. You'll be able to explore, discover, build things and play sports. You'll travel, swim, skydive, dance, go hiking, read books, play games, make music and do whatever other good thing your heart desires. You may even reign over the new creation as kings and queens.

Of course, this is only if you know Jesus. *"For there is salvation in no-one else! God has given no other name under heaven by which we must be saved."* (Acts 4:12) If you're an atheist, you have no such hope. As an atheist, death will ultimately render your life meaningless and even now, everything you do is currently fading away into oblivion, counting for nothing. Quite simply, outside of Jesus there is no life or purpose at all. And with that in mind, why reject him a second longer? Why not accept the sacrifice of the one who conquered death, and share in his inheritance of everlasting life? Why not do that right away?

The moment you confess with your lips that Jesus Christ is Lord and put your trust in him, you will pass from death to life, and everything sad will come untrue, and somehow it will all be even better for having once been broken and lost. God will find a way to use all things for good, and will work through your pain, your past mistakes and suffering to produce amazing fruit. And the best part of all? It's completely free. It's a free gift of grace. So again, why delay?

Christians, I hope this book has given you some fuel to help avoid being discouraged by life. Don't lose heart! If there's one thing that God has written into the structure of the universe it's that after even the darkest of nights, the morning *always* returns. After night comes day! Always! And it comes at the darkest moment too. So it will be with Jesus. God's written this concept into the seasons too. Every twelve months we watch the seasons turn and in the middle of winter, things can seem intolerably bleak, but Spring *always* returns! Life always returns, even from death. God is shouting to us through creation here. Summer is not a lie. He will return. And just because you can't see the sun right now, it doesn't mean it has ceased to exist. Take heart!

Don't get caught up in the world like everyone else. Money is useful inasmuch as it helps us to survive but don't worry about it or make it the sole focus of your life. You can't take it with you when you go so make sure while you have it, you invest it in the eternal kingdom of God. And don't settle for a mediocre, lukewarm faith either. Jesus is the only one through whom life has any meaning, so live it well for him. Arthur Schopenhauer wrote, *"What disturbs and depresses young people is the hunt for happiness on the firm assumption that it must be met within life. From this arises constantly deluded hope and so also dissatisfaction. Deceptive images of vague happiness hover before us in our dreams, and we search in vain for their original. Much would have been gained if, through timely advice and instruction, young people could have had eradicated from their minds the erroneous notion that the world has a great deal to offer them.*"3 This world is no longer meant to be the fulfilment of all your dreams. What you're looking for is up ahead, so live life within that context.

We tend to imagine that we're all due a minimum of 70 years and that we'll all get the chance to grow old. That's a false assumption and the truth is that many of us will be taken much sooner. Indeed, even as I write this very minute, a friend of a friend is attending a funeral for a 31 year old who has been taken through cancer. Therefore, knowing life is short and precious, live it in pursuit of worthy things. Follow God ordained dreams. Make your life count. Do the impossible. Make a difference in the lives of your fellow men. What does it matter if you perish in the attempt? You're going home anyway. Just try.

And finally, even though I've said it already a hundred times...don't lose heart! Don't lose heart! Don't. Just don't. The world needs courageous Christians more than anything today. If you see a brother or sister that is losing heart for some reason, then go help them to finish their race. Let's help each other towards the finish line. But don't lost heart! The world is hard and will get harder. The unravelling will go on for a while yet. But just as the chaos reaches its nadir, and we are tempted to give up and fall away, Jesus *will* return! He's going to make good on everything he promised. If he loved us enough to come to earth to die on a cross the first time, we can be sure he loves us enough to come get us when the time is right. The promised land is coming. Hold on. It will be worth it.

One day soon, we're all going home.

"...I am going to prepare a place for you...When everything is ready, I will come and get you, so that you will always be with me where I am." (John 14:2-3)

Epilogue

It's A Wonderful Life

My favourite film of all time is *It's A Wonderful Life* starring Jimmy Stewart and Donna Reed. If you haven't seen it and don't want to know what happens then skip this epilogue because it's got some spoilers! But for me, *It's A Wonderful Life* sums up the story of life more beautifully than any other movie I can think of.

The story begins with a young boy called George Bailey who has big dreams of what his life is going to look like. He dreams of adventure and wants to explore the world. It's all so fascinating and wonderful to him and he can't wait for the day when he grows up big enough to shake the dust off his sleepy little hometown (Bedford Falls) and go take it all in. Italy, Bermuda, New York, the Middle East...he's got it all in his sights.

By the time he grows up to be a young man, he's encountered a couple of little setbacks - perhaps the greatest of which was losing the hearing in one ear while saving his brother from an icy lake - but he's still full of the same ideals.

Talking to his father at the dinner table one evening, he tells him about his ambitions to go to college and what he'll do when he gets out. He says he's going to *"build things...design new buildings...plan modern cities."* His father has heard this wide-eyed optimism before: *"Still after that first million before your thirty"*, he says. George jokes he'll settle for half that in cash. But either way, he's got life all figured out. He's going to live out his dreams!

His father asks if he might want to just come back to Bedford Falls after college. He could settle down there and take a job in the family Building & Loan company. The Building & Loan doesn't make much money, but it does a lot of good for the local community, helping the working class residents to get on the property ladder and build a life for themselves.

George doesn't want to offend his father, who has given his own life to the company, but he can't stand the idea. *"Oh now, Pop, I couldn't. I couldn't face being cooped up for the rest of my life in a shabby little office."* The idea of just plugging into The System doing something he doesn't care for scares him. He says, *"This business of nickels and dimes and spending all your life trying to figure out how to save three cents on a length of pipe...I'd go crazy. I want to do something big and something important."* Surely life is too precious to spend cooped up in a small-town office? Referencing some of the early setbacks he's had, he comments how he's already slightly behind in his schedule for life: *"Most of my friends have already finished college. I just feel like if I don't get away, I'd bust!"*

Later that evening, George is at a school prom where he meets his future wife, Mary. The dancefloor is retractable and underneath is a newly installed swimming pool. As George and Mary dance, a couple of kids decide to play a trick on them by opening up the floor and causing George and Mary to fall into the water. Although completely drenched, with their clothes ruined, to them it's a just little left jab from life and nothing more. Their youthful joy and optimism completely overrides any frustration they might have felt. They take it all in their stride and start dancing in the pool, having even more fun than if they'd stayed dry. Their spirits just won't be crushed.

On the way home from the dance, George starts telling Mary about everything he's going to be. He tells her, *"I know what I'm going to do tomorrow and the next day and the year after that. I'm shaking the dust of this crummy little town off my feet, and I'm going to see the world! Italy, Greece, the Parthenon, the Coliseum. Then I'm coming back here and go to college and see what they know...and then I'm going to build things! I'm gonna build air fields. I'm gonna build skyscrapers a hundred storeys high! I'm gonna build bridges a mile long..."* George thinks he can do anything he wants and be anything he wants. Because life if just full of limitless possibilities. In fact, he's so confident that he says to Mary, *"What is it you want, Mary? What do you want? You want the moon? Just say the word and I'll throw a lasso around it and pull it down."* There's nothing he feels he can't do.

Over the course of time, life's blows begin to land on George and he is met with many disappointments. First his father dies suddenly. As a result of that, he can't go to college anymore. He has to stay behind in Bedford Falls and take his father's position at the Building & Loan company. He's doing the very thing he didn't want to do, counting nickels and dimes and working out how to save three cents on a length of pipe. Instead, he self-sacrificially gives his college money to his brother Harry, who goes off to get an education.

Four years go by while he waits for his brother Harry to come back from college. George is getting older now - he's in the full swing of adulthood, and the dream of getting an education has gone - but he still hopes that when Harry comes back to Bedford Falls, he'll take over the Building & Loan for a while so that he can be freed to finally do some travelling.

Noticeably by now, some of the heart has gone from him and his sights are set a little lower. He's no longer thinking about long-distance, trouble free tourism. Instead, he's focusing on finding jobs in less glamorous places, so that he can see some sights on the evenings and weekends. He tells his uncle Billy, *"There are plenty of jobs around for someone who likes to travel...Venezuela oil fields...the Yukon for someone who has engineering experience."* It's not quite what he dreamed about as a child, life is starting to beat him down a little bit, but his hope isn't completely dead yet.

When his brother Harry arrives home from college, it turns out he's now married and has been offered a great job working for his father-in-law. Harry can't hold the fort at the Building & Loan, meaning George isn't going to be able to get away at all. No travelling. Not even for work. He's stuck in Bedford Falls forever. It's another crushed dream.

Love however, comes at just the right time to give George a boost. He gets married to his teenage sweetheart, Mary, and with a bit of savings behind them, they're finally set to go travelling for their honeymoon. As they head to the airport, he excitedly tells Ernie the taxi driver about their plans: *"You know what we're going to do? We're going to shoot the works. A whole week in New York. A whole week in Bermuda. The highest hotels, the oldest champagne, the richest caviar, the hottest music, and the prettiest wife!"* Love has resuscitated some of the old optimism in George and things finally appear to be going his way. That's what love does.

However, just as they're about to leave Bedford Falls, the Great Depression hits. The townsfolk are all trying to withdraw their money from the banks, and from the Building & Loan too. This is potentially disastrous as it would mean the entire business going bankrupt and shutting down, the Bailey family all being out of work, and all those working folks who were scrimping and saving to build a better life for their families through the Building & Loan would be ruined. George saves the day by using all his honeymoon savings to keep the Building & Loan open and to feed the townsfolk until the crisis is over. Once again, his dream of travel has been met with disappointment.

Year after year goes by, and George gets older still. He watches as his friends go off to find prosperity and success in The System and when he compares his life to theirs, he feels miserable. Some of them relocate to New York and take exotic vacations to places he used to dream about as a boy, like Florida and Europe. And all the while he remains stuck in the crummy old town he despises, in an old draughty house, driving an old beat up car. He never gets his college education, he never gets to travel and he never gets to build skyscrapers or bridges. All his hopes and ambitions have been crushed. So much for all that childhood idealism he had.

He never gets close to making that million either by the way. In fact, he has to work long hours, scrimping and saving just to get by. And no matter how hard he works, the Building & Loan never generates enough to provide his wife or kids with the nice things he'd like to give them.

As if this weren't bad enough, World War II comes along, and causes the whole town to live under fear of invasion from Nazi Germany. Although George can't go to the frontline on account of his impaired hearing, it all impacts on the way he views the world. No longer is it a place of wide-eyed wonder. Instead, it's a place of evil and fear. And there is only relief when the whole thing passes by.

George is taking left jabs and right hooks every day. Eventually all the problems come to a head when a large sum of money is lost from the Building & Loan, and suddenly George has a threat of corruption charges hanging over his head. Even though it was an innocent mistake by his Uncle Billy, George's name will be scandalised, and what's more likely is that he could even be sent to jail on suspicion of embezzlement.

This is the last straw. If a life of broken dreams, disappointments, frustrations, drudgery in The System and war weren't enough, now he could spend the rest of his days behind bars. Feeling like a complete failure, and as though life really is a hopeless and eternal struggle, he has been beaten to his knees. Ain't nothing going to hit as hard as life.

He comes home from work that evening in a black hole of despair. The frustration he feels begins to boil over as he lashes out at his wife and kids, and then on the back of a blazing row, he heads to the bar to get drunk. Alcohol is his choice of coping mechanism to numb the pain in his heart. It's his anaesthetic. Life is hurting and he just doesn't want to feel anymore.

It's while he's at the bar that things start to turn around for him, for it's there that he makes the best decision he's ever made: He decides to reach out to God.

With tears in his eyes, he prays, *"God...God...Dear Father in Heaven, I'm not a praying man, but if you're up there and you can hear me, show me the way. I'm at the end of my rope. Show me the way, God."*

Instinctively, George returns to the first meaning of life: to know and live in relationship with his Creator. And God answers his prayer by sending an angel called Clarence to help. Just as he's about to throw himself off a bridge Clarence arrives and begins to show George what life would have been like for the people of Bedford Falls if he'd never been born. And it's bleak picture.

If George had never been born, his brother Harry would have died in the icy lake as a child because George wouldn't have been around to rescue him. Without either Harry or George, their mother would have been childless. The Building & Loan would have shut down after his father's death, meaning all the working class townsfolk would never have had the chance to own homes or build better lives. Mary would never have gotten married, and they would never have had any children. Furthermore, uncle Billy would have ended up in an asylum.

When George sees this vision, he realises that actually, although he didn't get to do the things that he wanted to do as a child, he's really had a wonderful life after all. He didn't make millions, or go to college, or travel the world, or design cities and bridges, but here's what he did do:

1. George turned to God. He prayed. And when he did, he discovered that God was there, ready to answer him. Before that plea for help, George Bailey hadn't been a praying man. After that moment however, he became a firm believer.

2. George had lived his life loving others in practical ways. He'd saved his brother's life and let him have his college money. He'd used his honeymoon money to keep a roof over the people's heads during the Great Depression. He had a wife and a family whom he loved and who loved him. He had a community of friends in Bedford Falls who had all benefitted from his kindness and generosity in some way and who all loved him for it.

3. He had spent his days in a worthy cause. He hadn't built skyscrapers or designed cities but through the Building & Loan, he had built homes for people who otherwise wouldn't have been able to afford it. And though he didn't personally get rich from it, he was making their lives better. Bedford Falls looked a little bit more like heaven as a result of his efforts.

The upshot? George Bailey discovered that the meaning of a wonderful life is threefold: to love God, love others, and to spend your life in a worthy cause. Sound familiar? It's what this whole book has really been about. To me, it encapsulates what life is all about. And that's why It's A Wonderful Life is my favourite movie of all time.

Let me just sum it all up if I can one more time: We come here with great expectations; great hopes and dreams; because we think we've come to Eden. We haven't. We've come to the world that sin has made, not the world that God originally intended for us. So we'll be met with disappointments - so many disappointments - and they will threaten to take the heart from us. But if we keep focused on what really matters - if we love God, love others, and spend our days in a worthy cause, we can make life better for those around us. We can help each other on the journey. We can change realities and we can alter eternities. And then, even through our trials, there will come a time when we'll arrive home, and discover even our worst moments were shaping us and fitting us for everlasting life. We'll discover that *"nothing can ever separate us from God's love. Neither death nor life, neither angels nor demons, neither our fears for today nor our worries about tomorrow - not even the powers of hell can separate us from God's love. No power in the sky or in the earth below - indeed nothing in all creation will ever be able to separate us from the love of God that is revealed in Christ Jesus our Lord." (Romans 8:38-39)*

You know, people often talk about the meaning of life as though it's the great unanswerable question, but it's right there in Genesis. If you love God, love others, and commit to live in pursuit of a worthy cause, then whatever else happens I can guarantee you'll have a pretty wonderful life. And at the end of it, an incredible eternity too.

You'll have found your way home.

To Inform, Inspire & Ignite

Other titles from this ministry include:

Know Your Enemy (DVD/EBook)
Exploring The New World Order From A Christian Perspective

Stay Free (DVD/Paperback/Ebook)
Why Society Can't Survive Without God

The Restless Church (DVD/Paperback/Ebook)
Rediscovering New Testament Christianity

**Revelation: The Fuel Project Guide
(DVD/Paperback/Ebook)**

**Answers: For A Postmodern Age
(DVD/Paperback/Ebook)**

To purchase, please visit the online store at thefuelproject.org. Alternatively, books and e-books can be found on Amazon, while DVDs are available from TheApologeticsGroup.com.

If you'd like to get in touch with The Fuel Project, email authenticfuel@gmail.com. You can also find the ministry on social media, including Facebook, Twitter, Instagram and YouTube.

If you'd like to donate to the work of this ministry, a link is provided at the website: thefuelproject.org. Alternatively you can donate via PayPal using the address: authenticfuel@gmail.com.

Thank you
Mark Fairley

Notes and References

Chapter 1 - Childhood

1. This is our design for Fruit Bran cereal. To illustrate our naivety, notice how we thought we could offer free watches (plus a 20% off coupon! And 10% extra free!) on a product that we had already decided to sell for less than £1!

2. Ecclesiastes 3:11

3. As reported in The Daily Mail, 30th January, 2014

Chapter 2 - Tweenagers

1. Charlie Brooker, The Guardian, 2nd June, 2014

2. Harvey (1950)

3. http://www.urbandictionary.com/define.php?term=tween

4.http://www.dcfchurch.org/Media/Player.aspx?media_id=1610
04&file_id=172702

5. The Guardian, November 27, 2015

6. Mere Christianity, CS Lewis

7. Genesis 1:26

8. Genesis 2:18

9. Genesis 1:28

10. Genesis 2:15

11. Genesis 1:28

12. Genesis 3:8-9

13. Brave New World Revisited, Aldous Huxley

14. Mere Christianity, CS Lewis

15. Garden State (2004)
http://www.imdb.com/title/tt0333766/quotes

16. John 14:3

17. John 11:25-26

18. Revelation 21:5

19. Matthew 19:14

Chapter 3 - The Mid Teens

1. Of Human Bondage, W. Somerset Maugham

2. Rocky Balboa (2006)

3. http://www.independent.co.uk/life-style/health-and-families/health-news/number-of-children-who-self-harm-jumps-70-per-cent-in-just-two-years-9660478.html

4. http://jasonfoundation.com/prp/facts/youth-suicide-statistics/

5. http://www.qotd.org/search/search.html?aid=944&page=2

Chapter 4 - The Late Teens

1. Definition by Dictionary.com

2.http://www.brainyquote.com/quotes/quotes/j/jeffbridge318881.html

3. http://www.goodreads.com/quotes/tag/cynicism

4. http://www.scrapbook.com/quotes/doc/14545.html

5.http://www.brainyquote.com/quotes/keywords/cynicism.html

6. http://www.goodreads.com/quotes/tag/cynicism

7. Helen Keller (http://www.goodreads.com/quotes/9605-life-is-either-a-daring-adventure-or-nothing-at-all)

Chapter 5 - Young Adulthood

1. As noted in William Wilberforce: The Life Of The Great Anti-Slave Trade Campaigner by William Hague

2. http://www.goodreads.com/quotes/1020919-god-almighty-has-set-before-me-two-great-objects-the

3. William Wilberforce p.272

4. William Wilberforce p.276

5. William Wilberforce: A Biography by Stephen Tomkins

6. http://www.goodreads.com/quotes/1089482-believe-no-pessimist-ever-discovered-the-secrets-of-the-stars

7. Speech delivered 28 August, 1963 at the Lincoln Memorial in Washington DC.

(http://www.americanrhetoric.com/speeches/mlkihaveadream.htm)

8.The young's lack of conformity to reality is also what tends to make them the most inventive musicians, film-makers, writers, artists, photographers, engineers, scientists and whatever else. A poor grasp of reality, or at least the status quo, can be a fantastic thing.

9. Katie's story is chronicled in "Kisses From Katie"

10. http://www.goodreads.com/quotes/311003-i-grew-up-with-an-ambition-and-determination-without-which

11. The Impossible Dream by Mitch Leigh and Joe Darion

Chapter 6 - Adulthood

1. Stats from Alcohol Concern (https://www.alcoholconcern.org.uk/help-and-advice/statistics-on-alcohol)

2. Stats from Foundation For A Drug Free World. (http://www.drugfreeworld.org/drugfacts/alcohol/international-statistics.html)

3. Various sources as quoted in the Huffington Post (http://www.huffingtonpost.com/kelly-fitzgerald/15-shocking-alcohol-stati_b_7010680.html)

4. http://www.goodreads.com/quotes/11589-i-have-absolutely-no-pleasure-in-the-stimulants-in-which

5. Cited on Google bio for Edgar Allen Poe

6. http://www.goodreads.com/quotes/368731-we-must-not-cease-from-exploration-and-the-end-of

7. The Peace of Wild Things by Wendell Berry (Poem)

8. http://www.goodreads.com/quotes/423137-why-are-we-worn-out-why-do-we-who-start

9. "I Dreamed A Dream" From the musical Les Miserables is a great song that sums up the disillusionment that can come from life. There was no place to fit this into the main body of the book but hopefully reading the lyrics here will resonate:

"There was a time when men were kind
When their voices were soft
And their words inviting
There was a time when love was blind
And the world was a song
And the song was exciting
There was a time when it all went wrong...

I dreamed a dream in time gone by
When hope was high and life worth living
I dreamed that love would never die
I dreamed that God would be forgiving
Then I was young and unafraid
And dreams were made and used and wasted
There was no ransom to be paid
No song unsung, no wine untasted

But the tigers come at night
With their voices soft as thunder
As they tear your hopes apart
As they turn your dreams to shame

Still I dream he'd come to me
And we would live the years together
But there are dreams that cannot be
And there are storms we cannot weather

I had a dream that life would be
So different from this hell I'm living
So different now from what it seemed
Now life has killed the dream I dreamed.

Chapter 7 - Growing Old

1. Mere Christianity by CS Lewis
2. https://www.goodreads.com/author/quotes/6452394.Jackson_Burnett
3. From MacBeth by William Shakespeare
4. Article from The Telegraph, 4 February, 2016: ONS suicide statistics: 10 ways we can stop me killing themselves
5. As quoted: http://rzim.org/global-blog/is-paris-burning
6. If you'd like to read more inspiring stories of Christians who approached persecution and death in the same way as Paul and Stephen, I recommend the book Jesus Freaks, compiled by the Christian organisation Voice of the Martyrs.

I'm also reminded of something Frederich Buechner once wrote on this issue: *"The love for equals is a human thing—of friend for friend, brother for brother. It is to love what is loving and lovely. The world smiles.*

The love for the less fortunate is a beautiful thing—the love for those who suffer, for those who are poor, the sick, the failures, the unlovely. This is compassion, and it touches the heart of the world.

The love for the more fortunate is a rare thing—to love those who succeed where we fail, to rejoice without envy with those who rejoice, the love of the poor for the rich, of the black man for the white man. The world is always bewildered by its saints.

And then there is the love for the enemy—love for the one who does not love you but mocks, threatens, and inflicts pain. The tortured's love for the torturer. This is God's love. It conquers the world." (From The Magnificent Defeat)

Chapter 8 - Going Home

1.http://www.brainyquote.com/quotes/quotes/m/muhammadal148629.html

2. Beyond The Shadowlands: CS Lewis on Heaven and Hell

3. http://www.goodreads.com/quotes/369018-what-disturbs-and-depresses-young-people-is-the-hunt-for

Epilogue

It's A Wonderful Life (1946), Dir: Frank Capra

Made in the USA
San Bernardino, CA
06 October 2016